# Stop in the Name of Love

# Stop in the Name of Love

*Positive and Solution-Oriented
Behavior Interventions*

Noel R. Love

# Table of Contents

# Come on In

Come one and come all
To this tome of good will
Idea and suggestion
Intended to fill

To honor your work
That which you have learned
High prices paid
Wisdom hard earned

With children still growing
Some short and some tall
Some broken; some bruised
You strive to reach all

So, here you are
This book in your hand
An unwavering swimmer
In view of dry land

Some quit in deep water
Too tired, loss of hope
Through storm-driven waters
You pitched others the rope

You teach all our children
You nurture the seed
It is time someone tells you
You are just what we need

*"The human story does not always unfold like a mathematical calculation on the principle that two and two make four. Sometimes in life they make five or minus three; and sometimes the blackboard topples down in the middle of the sum and leaves the class in disorder and the pedagogue with a black eye."*
**Winston Churchill**

# Foreword

Considering all that is known and unknown, how a child behaves probably makes sense. This does not make it acceptable, but it does suggest there are reasons. This book speaks to anyone who works or associates with youth. Whether a classroom teacher, mental health counselor, probation officer, youth minister, or parent, addressing behavior is an essential component of what you do. Anyone can benefit from the pragmatic skills and effective strategies threaded throughout this book. We will look at the influences that affect behavior, such as family systems, depression, trauma and chemical involvement. We will look at a section on the skills needed to accomplish the job. We will look at vital information needed to facilitate an intervention and deal with patterns of acting out behavior.

As professionals, we most often see little more than the tip of the iceberg. Yet, we know that ninety percent of the iceberg is hidden and unseen. How a young person behaves is the tip; why a young person acts out is significant, though often unknown. We do not always see the trauma, yet it is there. The primary goal of this book is to provide common sense content that can be accessed and applied easily.

Dealing with resistant, inappropriate or acting out behavior is not why you chose to teach, counsel, mentor, supervise or parent kids. Very little time in college was devoted to discipline or classroom management; the parents who once fully backed the teacher now point their finger and claim unfairness. Behavior once seldom seen now occurs regularly and the time spent dealing with acting out behavior takes away from the time for instruction. The purpose of this intervention book is to offer effective tools to assist in behavior interventions.

This book is for those who regularly intervene with students whose behaviors are self-defeating and disruptive to the learning environment. Whether repetitive, periodic or isolated, acting out in the classroom requires effective and at times imaginative responses. Written as an intervention resource, this book contains information on the dynamics that contribute to acting out and what can be done. It is not an academic intervention resource; the intent is to help you address kids who are acting out in the classroom, church, hallway, cafeteria, gymnasium, parking lot, neighborhood or home.

# Acknowledgements

Donna, if I added up all my spoken and unspoken words dedicated to you, they would still fall far short of expressing my love and gratitude. Though it is cliché, I want to thank you for the tremendous and unwavering support and encouragement. This book would not exist without your support. Thanks for sharing your heart, soul and life with me.

Mom and dad, whether through DNA, modeling, or rearing, thank you for the gift of loving to read and write; it truly is a gift that keeps on giving. The pleasure I get from writing pulses deep inside. I appreciate your tolerance when ninth grade English almost deadened the joy.

I also want to recognize two people who had more to do with this book than they will ever truly know: Don Clark, who embodies the philosophy of positive thinking in the most courageous and contagious way I know of. Don, I never got tired of you asking me if this book was done. Also, Elizabeth Clark, who showed that there are no obstacles that cannot be overcome. Her unwavering perseverance and determination did not so much push me as inspire. The expression of gratitude and appreciation exceeds my vocabulary and eloquence. I fall short of articulating what you two have meant in my life.

# A Word about References and Sources

You will find some information that I used to support a statement. Most was public information from the government, a few from universities and even less from independent research. Though you will find acknowledgements, I mostly leaned on what I learned throughout my career. Many readers will understand. A person can spend years devoted to what he or she does, learn an incredible amount of information or techniques, and possess little more than a clue where they originated. To include every reference or resource used, I would have to recognize the hundreds of parents who sought my assistance, wringing their hands in worry and fear, wiping away tears of broken hearts, and wondering if their parenting had anything to do with the problem. They taught me well.

> *"Let us put our minds together and see what life we can make for our children."*
> **Sitting Bull**

# Bad Things do happen to Good Kids
# Part 1

Bad things sometimes happen to good kids, and sometimes, good kids do bad things. In Trish's case, both pertain. You see, Trish is a good kid. In fact, she is kind, thoughtful and gentle, a sweet child. Before she even started kindergarten, bad things did happen to Trish, very bad things. You may not know Trish by name, but within time, this damaged and broken child will come your way. She will be a problem in classrooms all over this country.

The closet is dark. The closet is where Trish hides, under a pile of soiled clothes. She sleeps there the night of her sixth birthday. She is frightened. She knows not even a special day such as her birthday can keep her safe. Trish is not alone in the closet; she is holding her little brother Jimmy, telling him in a trembling and troubled voice that things will be okay. The words should be comforting, but her tone is not. She has said those words before; they just did not help much. Last night, she drifted to sleep holding Jimmy's hand. Like so many nights before she slept fitfully and had very bad dreams.

Though the closet is pitch dark, Trish knows Jimmy is crying because of the constant sniffling and hitching of his breath. They hear footsteps. Trish whispers to Jimmy to hold his breath as long as he can. She does the same. She needs to be brave for her little brother. Trish prays that Jimmy keeps quiet as long as Donald, their stepfather, is in the house. Donald's face turns red and veins pop out on his neck; he screams, kicks, hits and turns into a real-life monster.

Both cringe every time they hear the resounding slap of his hand on their mother's face. It is more than the sound of the slaps that frighten the children. Donald curses and sometimes hits her in the mouth; he becomes mean and terrifying when he drinks. Trish knows that mom tries to hide the swollen eyes, facial bruises and busted lips. Trish has never said anything to mom about the beating. She can tell mom is ashamed. Trish knows that after Donald beats mom, the three of them will act as if it never happened. Just like last year, Trish's birthday will again go by without much fanfare.

While huddled in the dark, Trish tries to wipe away the tears rolling down her cheeks. She has learned to cry in silence and in solitude.

This morning, Trish feels lucky that she and Jimmy have the closet in which to hide. At her young age, she is not aware that other children do not sleep in their closets. After all, "aren't all families like hers?" she wonders. When she is older and learns the truth, Trish will not like the answer to that question at all. She is aware that now little Jimmy is holding her hand. His hand is so tiny, so small. Even while asleep, he squeezes so tightly. She makes him feel safe. They listen and hear nothing. They again hold their breath so they don't make a sound. They have to be very sure Donald is gone before risking even a peak out the door. They made that mistake before, and Trish swears she will never let her little brother get hit and kicked again. It is not always in a dream that a monster chases her. When he is angry, Donald's eyes are also empty, black and cold. The difference is that he doesn't fade away when she opens her eyes. Trish prefers her nightmares.

Suddenly the door opens and the kids freeze. If Trish and Jimmy do not move a muscle, or make a sound, maybe the monster will go away. To their overwhelming relief, they hear mom's voice whispering their names. This means it is safe to come out. The kids can breathe again. Thank God for the daytime. Thank God for mom. Thank God for closets. Outside a hard rain begins to fall, pelting the windows with large drops of water. Skies darken, lightning strikes and thunder rolls.

Trish looks up from under her treasured pile of filthy clothes and sees mom smiling. What a relief, sort of. She sees mom dimly smile through swollen, bruised eyes, and bloodied, cracked lips. Mom sits down, pulls both Trish and Jimmy toward her and begins to rock back and forth quietly singing the "Happy Birthday" song. In a voice as hollow as her heart and her hopes, mom says; "Happy birthday honey, it's going to be a wonderful day. After school, we are going to the zoo. Maybe they've finished the new exhibits and the lions and bears are no longer caged." Mom says one more thing before she leaves the room: "Don't you just hate seeing those poor animals all caged up?"

That day the rain falls, the sky cracks, the thunder explodes, hope fades, promises are broken, and Trish sinks deeper into her own kind of cage. Trish knows that later the monster with empty eyes will be back. He never leaves for very long. She wishes he would. Leaving the closet, Trish catches her reflection in her mirror and asks herself; "When do I get out of my cage?" She dresses for school, catches the bus and quietly sits at her desk on the back row. She is one of your students and you know nothing at all about any of this. You see a quiet, sweet, gentle and caring child. In time, Trish will change. You see, bad things do happen to good kids and sometimes good kids do bad things.

# Part 2

**Continued on page 269**

# Section 1

## Realizing the Change

*"Character cannot be developed in ease and quiet. Only through experience of trial and suffering can the soul be strengthened," vision cleared, ambition inspired, and success achieved."*
**Helen Keller**

# Winter Winds

Winter winds are upon us
Scattered dead leaves
Of the wind no containment
Around us empty stark trees

Yet, in the promise of tomorrow
Something vibrant and green
In the dark night around us
We welcome the spring

The fragrance of summer
Lingers fresh in the air
Bare feet crosses meadows
With hardly a care

Hot sun brings us memories
Of finding cool shade
Long days of baked earth
Slowly light fades

With shortened days cooler
Green leaves they turn brown
Then fall from the trees
Without making sound

We prepare for the cold time
Shivering we wait
Those brown leaves are piled up
Gone is their fate

Where do they end up
Those piles in the lawn
With cold wind now upon us
The circle goes on

*"It is not the strongest of the species that survive, nor the most intelligent, but the one most responsive to change."*
**Author unknown, commonly misattributed to Charles Darwin**

# Chapter 1

# Why do we Need Intervention?

Taking into consideration the real and dramatic changes that have occurred in our society, we can begin to understand why some of our children come to school with little or no social skills. Rudeness, insults, attacks, undermining and meanness are seen, heard and felt on a daily basis. Mass media and popular culture seems to thrive on digging for new lows year after year. What would have absolutely shocked our grandparents is now routinely seen. Most likely, in another twenty years, the norm will be so far beyond today that many of us will be shocked. I imagine many of us are shocked today!

## Changes Come About

*"If we could still use corporal punishment, things would be better!"*
*"I wish students could still sit in the corner with a dunce hat on!"*
*"A good smack on the knuckle never hurt anyone!"*

The above statements reflect a wishful, yet naïve belief that the tools and techniques that worked in the past are just as effective with children in the present when addressing behavior. Of course, this does not refer to every skill or tool. There are strategies that were effective then and remain so today. And, there are many that no longer have the efficacy once enjoyed. In every school, there are faculty members who cling onto what is familiar; they hang onto the old school techniques. We all establish a comfort zone and prefer to stay there. We tend to establish a routine and resist change.

It is hard to think of another industry where change and upgrades are resisted so fiercely. For example, it is understood that a school cannot function like a car repair shop, yet there is an interesting contrast. In the last thirty years, mechanics have had to struggle to keep up with changes in cars, particularly in the arena of computer technology. Yet, there is not a mechanic around who could make a living holding tight to the old ways (unless he restores classics, of course). Under normal conditions, it would be career suicide to ignore or refuse to progress with the changes. Schools do not change with the same urgency, and subsequently many tools from yesterday don't work today.

The degree of information needed to recognize many of the reasons students act out is included in this book. What professional doesn't need to understand depression, loss or trauma? We are not expected to become experts in every factor of a student's life; we just need to understand that kids rarely ask for the trauma in their lives. We are all given a hand to play, some are Aces and others are all Jokers.

> ### Statements sometimes heard in school and home:
>
> *"For the last time, I'm telling you to get in your seat! Don't make me say it again; you don't want me to have to come over there. Do you hear me, mister?"*
>
> *"I've had it up to here. Last night was the last straw; I'm contacting that military school today."*
>
> *"I have no idea what to do with this one. Everything I tried seems to fall on deaf ears. I just wish she wasn't in my fourth period class."*
>
> *"He's your kid, you do something with him. I am over it."*

The term intervention applies to a number of different situations; but, the primary purpose is to interrupt behavior, offer alternatives, restore learning or provide an opportunity for a major change. *Interrupting* behavior is the same as *intervention* as it is approached in this book. Regardless of the setting and situation, the tools contained in this "toolbox" are helpful and offered in hopes you will find the contents beneficial. Interventions are examined from the win-win perspective where all participants walk away satisfied with the outcome.

The style and techniques of intervening will not be based on an authoritarian model, or a power base. It has been established that power-based (I win-you lose) interventions do not work well. Adults have butted heads with kids for years with a no-win situation evolving. Also, this book will not discuss interventions that include bribing, pleading, preaching, shaming or manipulating. Overall, the approach to intervention in this book will be positive, solution-oriented and will offer a win-win outcome for all. Teacher's and other professionals can address inappropriate behavior and still support the learning process.

## Clear Intensions

Outside of the education field, formal interventions have been effectively facilitated since the early 1970's. Professionals from the chemical dependency field have worked with families to ultimately get a loved one such as an alcoholic parent or drug dependent daughter help. The intervention melted the icy denial most often experienced with this particular disease. An effective family intervention serves as a "mirror" that accurately reflects what is happening. Family interventions are fueled by love; strong emotions such as hurt, loss, confusion, rejection, resentment and fear are expressed. When facilitated effectively (usually with a skilled interventionist) these interventions worked more than 80% of the time. The person experiencing the intervention ends up seeing the negative impact on others and agrees to take the appropriate action. Interventions structured in this fashion restore families and save lives.

Historically, employers have used interventions as a way of leveraging an employee into making a decision, such as entering treatment. Judges have intervened from the bench when a legal consequence is used to "force" a person into getting help. Though it originated to address chemical dependency, interventions can be used in a number of situations in school.

In referencing the emotional components of family interventions, we can better contrast how school-based interventions differ. The school's leverage isn't love, the law or one's employment. The leverage is the language, style and intent in which an intervention is provided. The application of strategies presented will enable you to intervene effectively and skillfully. We will look at interventions from several angles including interventions conducted by the classroom teacher, administrator, intervention team and even the family.

Interventions can be planned and structured events with a specific outcome in mind, or a spontaneous interaction with a student who needs redirection. Both of these are addressed in this book. If you are a member of a student assistance early intervention team, a teacher, administrator, or a frustrated parent, this book is for you. Certainly, attempts to interrupt behavior fail. They can fall flat or even instigate more acting out. Intervention and confrontation are not necessarily the same things. The term "confrontation" often implies that you have to solidly plant your feet, stand in someone's face, put hands on your hips and speak loudly. In this book, "confrontation" means facing a person by addressing the behavior, not the student. While giving support to the person, we will look at ways to quickly, effectively intervene, with dignity. It is true that we can draw flies with sugar, rather than vinegar. Another way of expressing the approach of this book is to say we are going to intervene while treating others the way we want to be treated—with dignity, respect and honesty.

*"It takes no more time being thoughtful and caring than it takes to be a jerk."*
**Anonymous**

## What Used to be No Longer Is!

In the 1950's students were asked to list the problems that most often interfered with learning or were observed at school. The same question is asked of students today. The comparison is below:

| 1950's | 2000's | |
|---|---|---|
| *Talking* | *Alcohol* | *Drugs* |
| *Chewing gum* | *Assault* | *Gangs* |
| *Making noise* | *Murder* | *STD's* |
| *Running in halls* | *Pregnancy* | *Burglary* |
| *Cutting in line* | *Suicide* | *Rape* |
| *Breaking dress code* | *Vandalism* | *Extortion* |
| *Not putting paper in trash* | **Terrorism** | **Bullying** |

No matter how we look at it, the fabric of our society has unraveled and appears unchecked. With increasing momentum, the things we once took for granted seem to dissolve into a flood of financial, emotional, social and spiritual decay or bankruptcy. Estimates are that more than one-fourth of all children will be born into single-parent households living in poverty. More than half of our students will experience their parents' divorce. Sexual abuse occurs so frequently that studies estimate that more than one third of our children will be touched inappropriately by an adult, often someone they should be able to trust. Parental alcoholism directly affects a quarter of our student population and violent, random crimes have reached the most secure neighborhoods. Handguns kill more children than illnesses do. Only drunk driving kills more.

This disturbing litany of changes troubles the most stoic among us. To teach children can be at times demoralizing, and healthy skepticism can threaten to turn into rank cynicism. Effective interventions offer us an opportunity to contradict this sense of discouragement by giving us tools to help youth in at-risk situations. It gives us the ability to redirect behavior and motivate positive decisions and subsequently changes.

*While gazing at the stars, one enlightened man said to his friend with boastful pride, "I've decided to accept the universe as it is." His common-sensed friend replied with an incredulous,*
**"My God, what other choice is there?"**

We really have no choice but to accept how much things have changed. Wishing and lamenting about the "old days" doesn't make it so. Hoping to return to those days when the three R's ruled the classroom is naïve. Just ask members of certain ethnic groups or women about returning to yesteryear. I suspect there is some euphoric recall when people pine for "the olden days". It appears to be greener when grown in the past.

## Bad or Wounded?

One would hope the answer to this question is obvious, but it isn't for some adults who work with students that "act bad". How many times has something like this been said, "He's just a bad seed. That boy has got the devil inside him!" If so, we beg to ask at what age did the boy become intrinsically bad? Was he born bad, or wired in such a way that he always will be trouble? As a baby, did he give the "evil eye" or project vomit on mom or dad? The "terrible two's" may be tough, but I doubt we can say she's "just a bad child". It is probably his DNA, right?

This book approaches acting out or "messing up" from the perspective that all children are born good and delightful. They are sweet, gentle, soft, happy and curious (even you and me). An infant lives in the here-and-now and is unblemished by trauma or loss. Then baby begins to slowly lose that "natural" state of serenity and joy. As he continues to grow and age, scars emerge from life's traumas such as death, divorce or abuse. The toddler begins to learn "facts" often based on the dysfunction of the previous generations. He questions his self-worth and wonders what is wrong with him. He learns the world is not such a trusting place. He spends a lot of time somewhere else in his head, maybe where things aren't so wrong. The toddler has become a troubled child; you might say he's gone from diapers to destruction.

By the time he gets to school, it has already happened. His self-talk is negative. He doesn't like to play with others. He seems to have a mean streak and is very obstinate for such a young child. Who knows why? It would take a crystal ball to understand him. Is this a bad kid who makes trouble, or a good kid living through trouble? Regardless, we need to be willing to separate the person from the behavior, so that the child is supported and the behavior addressed. And, to think this was the "sweet, gentle, soft, happy and curious" baby we all loved so much.

There will always be some who will resist new things such as refusing to re-sharpen the saw blade. The comfort zone does feel safer! For the rest of us, making changes or adjustments are opportunities to upgrade the tool kit. That willingness, filtered by need, caution and a slight skepticism (not all tools are needed) is the key to the utilization of this book.

Before looking specifically at interventions, we need to first consider why students need interventions in the first place. By taking an insightful look at the underlying reasons for certain behaviors, our understanding increases. As a person understands these problems, empathy and concern increases. With any insight at all to trauma, addiction, loss, or family systems, a person cannot help but see each child as intrinsically good.

> *"He may act badly, but that doesn't make him so.*
> *Hate the sin; love the sinner."*
> **Anonymous**

## Still Accountable

There is an important point to make before going further. Looking at reasons why students act out is not an attempt to excuse anything. Accountability needs to apply except maybe in the most extreme situations such as a true psychosis. No matter the reasons, students still have to be accountable. Unfortunately, some adults have confused the words "reason" and "excuse" resulting in an intolerant, self-righteous posture that leaves very little room for empathy. People do make mistakes. By removing accountability a soft place to fall is created; people do need to answer for their actions. Let's first ensure we are on the same page with the following two words:

---

### Different Words Different Meaning

**Reason**—legitimate influences that impact behavior. *"I understand why he's having a real bad day; his grandfather died last night. He needs extra help right now."*

**Excuse**—a way to relinquish responsibility for a behavior. *"Poor thing, his grandfather died last night so I'll let him get away with it this time. He can't help himself."*

---

Kids do not start out with the life goal of being oppositional, dependent, lost, angry, or confused. They aren't hoping to become a disappointment to parents, a problem in school or a scourge in their neighborhood. At two, she's adorable; at thirteen she is spoken to with profanity, and at eighteen she's lost in the dark shadows. Our little one is on her way to becoming a shadow person who hovers on the fringes-out of sight, out of mind. What went wrong? Kids want to be loved and treated with respect like adults do. Most children don't have the articulate insights to express this in healthy ways (like adults do). Through behavior, attitude and decisions, students often paint themselves into a corner. Many students either feel defeated with head hung low and slouched posture or snarl in defense exposing jagged claws and sharp teeth. Interventions are a way to pull them out of that corner and offer a chance to return to the path that leads to a place where opportunities to succeed exist. There is no guarantee of this happening; all you can do is your best. No matter what the outcome, interventions are righteous. Any time we can reach out and grab a kid's hand before he or she sinks into the quicksand, we must! How could we not? Some might ask, "Why a book on intervention"? The answer is self-evident to those of us who are willing to take a closer, objective look.

The following story is a perfect way to enter into the world of interventions. I came across it years ago, as I was reading a publication entitled, "*The Way of Social Action.*" I have not been able to determine the author to commend. As you will observe, interventions take many shapes, some planned and some spontaneous, and some that are quite surprising. Enjoy!

## The Laborer and the Old Man

### Author Unknown

The train clanked and rattled through the suburbs of Tokyo on a drowsy spring afternoon. Our car was comparatively empty-a few housewives with their kids in tow and some old folks going shopping. I gazed absently at the drab houses and dusty hedgerows. At one station the doors opened and suddenly the afternoon quiet was shattered by a man bellowing violent, incomprehensible curses. The man staggered into our car. He wore laborers clothes and he was big, drunk and dirty. Screaming, he swung at a woman holding a baby. The blow sent her spinning into the laps of an elderly couple. It was a miracle that the baby was unharmed. Terrified, the couple jumped up and scrambled toward the other end of the car. The laborer aimed a kick at the retreating back of the old woman, but missed as they scuttled to safety. This so enraged the drunk that he grabbed the metal pole in the center of the car and tried to wrench it out of its place. I could see that one of his hands was cut and bleeding. The train lurched ahead, the passengers frozen with fear. I stood up.

I was young then, some twenty years ago, and in pretty good shape. I'd been putting in a solid eight hours of Aikido training nearly every day for the past three years. I like to throw and grapple. I thought I was tough. The trouble was my martial art skill was untested in actual combat. As students of Aikido, we were not allowed to fight. "Aikido," my teacher had said again and again, 'is the art of reconciliation'. Whoever has the mind to fight has broken his connection to the universe. If you try to dominate people, you are already defeated. We study how to resolve conflict, not how to start it."

I listened to his words. I tried hard. Earlier in the day I even went so far as to cross the street to avoid the punks who lounged around the train station. My forbearance exalted me. I felt both tough and holy. In my heart, however, I wanted an absolutely legitimate opportunity whereby I might save the innocent by destroying the guilty.

"This is it", I said to myself as I got to my feet. "People are in danger. If you don't do something fast, somebody will probably get hurt." Seeing me stand up, the drunk recognized a chance to focus his rage. "Aha!" he roared. "A foreigner!" You need a lesson in Japanese manners!" I held on lightly to the commuter strap overhead and gave him a slow look of disgust and dismissal. I planned to take this guy apart, but he had to make the first move. I wanted him mad, so I pursed my lips and blew him an insolent kiss. "All right!" he hollered. "You're going to get a lesson." He gathered himself for a rush at me.


A fraction of a second before he could move, someone shouted "Hey!" It was earsplitting. I remember the strangely joyous, lilting quality of it—as though you and a friend had been searching diligently for something, and he had suddenly stumbled upon it. "Hey!" I wheeled to my left; the drunk spun to his right. We both stared down at a little old Japanese man. He must have been well into his seventies, this tiny gentleman, sitting there immaculate in his kimono. He took no notice of me, but beamed delightedly at the laborer, as though he had a most important, most welcome secret to share.

"C'mere," the old man said in an easy vernacular, beckoning to the drunk. "C'mere and talk with me." He waved his hand lightly. The man followed, as if on a string. He planted his feet belligerently in front of the old gentleman, and roared above the clacking wheels, "Why the hell should I talk with you?" The drunk now had his back to me. If his elbow moved so much as a millimeter, I'd drop him in his socks. The old man continued to beam at the laborer. "Whatcha' been drinkin?" He asked, his eyes sparkling with interest. "I been drinkin" Sake," the laborer bellowed back, "and it's none of your business!" Flecks of spit spattered the old man.


"Oh, that's wonderful," the old man said, "absolutely wonderful." You see, I love Sake too. Every night, me and my wife, we warm up a little bottle of Sake and take it out into the garden, and sit on an old wooden bench. We watch the sun go down, and we look to see how our persimmon tree is doing. My great-grandfather planted that tree, and we worry about whether it will recover from the ice storms we had last winter. Our tree has done better than I expected though, especially when we consider the poor quality of the soil. It is gratifying to watch when we drink our Sake and go out to enjoy the evening—even when it rains!" He looked up at the laborer, eyes twinkling.

As he struggled to follow the old man's conversation, the drunk's face began to soften. He slowly unclenched his jaw. "Yeah," he said. "I love persimmons too . . ." His voiced trailed off. "Yes," said the old man, smiling, "and I'm sure you have a wonderful wife."

"No!" replied the laborer. "My wife died." Very gently, swaying with the motion of the train, the big man began to sob. "I don't got a wife, I don't got a home, and I don't got a job. I'm so ashamed of myself." Tears rolled down his cheek, a spasm of despair rippled through his body.

Now it was my turn. Standing there in my well-scrubbed, youthful innocence, my make-the-world-safe-for-democracy-righteousness, I suddenly felt dirtier that he was. The train arrived at my stop. As the door opened, I heard the old man cluck sympathetically. "My, my," he said. "That is a difficult predicament, indeed. Sit down here and tell me about it." I turned my head for one last look. The laborer was sprawled on the seat, his head in the old man's lap. The old man was softly stroking his filthy, matted hair.

As the train pulled away, I sat down on a bench. What I had wanted to do with muscle had been accomplished with kind words. I had just seen Aikido tried in combat, and the essence of it was love. I would have to practice the art with an entirely different spirit. It would be a long time before I could speak about the resolution of conflict.

*"The direct use of force is such a poor solution to any problem; it is generally employed only by small children and large nations."*
**David Friedman**

*"The problem is not that there are problems. The problem is expecting otherwise and thinking that having problems is a problem."*
**Theodore Ruben**

# Chapter 2

# A Reason for Everything

Understanding critical information leads to empathy, which is a vital aspect of successful interventions. This section will examine a number of issues that pertain to "why" students behave in inappropriate ways. If we consider all we know and all we don't know about a child, what he does probably makes sense; it doesn't excuse him, but it often answers the question "why". Everything happens for a reason, whether we see it or not.

*We're not in our places with bright shiny faces.*
*And this is not the way to start a new day.*

## Oh, How Things Have Changed!

There has never been a time when kids didn't experience trauma. One hundred years ago sexual abuse existed; but, children had no rights whatsoever and it was not discussed. Death of a parent or sibling was as common then as now. Alcohol and other drugs existed at that time, but we were not accustomed to the extent and widespread acceptance that student drug use was a right of passage. The list of social ills can go on and on, but let's stop making that list. No one wants to see an autopsy on society; it stinks too much.

Instead, let's look in on the "typical" classroom and see twenty five or more students and one teacher. Of these twenty five kids, experience reveals that six live in a home with a chemically dependent parent, eight have been or will be sexually abused by their senior year and twelve will see their mom and dad split up for good. In that same class, three will become chemically dependent, two will experience profound depression and fifteen will experience situational depression severe enough to impact their lives. We will see kids who will get pregnant out of wedlock, catch sexually transmitted diseases, see friends die from drunk driving and some may even witness a classmate die by violence.

This is not an attempt to over dramatize the situation; this would imply exaggeration. This classroom is not an exaggeration. Sadly, it is the typical classroom in many communities. Add to these traumatic situations, some of these students will stress out over standardized testing, cringe in fear of bullying behavior and grow sick and tired of the multiple transitions from one community to another. So, are we all in our places with bright shiny faces? I don't think so!

It would take a person who is a combined teacher, therapist, lawyer, nutritionist, family counselor, doctor and spiritual advisor to be adequately prepared for who comes through the classroom doors. Instead of approaching all of the problems we see, this section will look at how any kind of trauma impacts learning. In addition, we will look at why we see kids behave in ways that are clearly self-defeating and regardless of imposed consequences keep doing it.

Some of our students implode, withdraw, isolate, self mutilate, and give up. Others dig in, grab onto that which is most defiant, puff up with anger and defensiveness and work overtime to make teaching a daily fight. With some students, their choice is boiled down to giving up or acting out, or getting angry at self or at someone else.

It is estimated that ninety-five percent of American families are dysfunctional. Even if we cut that in half, we are still looking at a huge number of kids who go home to a situation that hurts instead of heals. What should be protective is now an at-risk factor. For some, waking up consists of no breakfast, unprepared home work, and poor performance in class. In the afternoon these kids may go home to an empty apartment, have no food to eat, no physical or emotional nourishment or love to soak up. Where is the sanctuary?

*"The average man does not want to be free. He simply wants to be safe."*
**H. L. Menken**

## This is Sanctuary?

Well, let's see; we have sex, alcohol and drugs. We have gangs to replace what isn't available in the family. Television serves as a babysitter to many and a sewer for most. Those with the means are able to lose themselves in electronic games. Some have a worn path from the couch to the refrigerator with no structure or limitations on what they eat. Exploding weight gain is happening for one third of our kids and a percentage of kids are experiencing rapid weight loss. Body images are distorted by Madison Avenue marketers and health care is unavailable to the neediest.

*"Their understanding begins to swell and the approaching tide will shortly fill the reasonable shores that now lie foul and muddy."*
**William Shakespeare**

## Painting a Picture

Sad, hurt, scared, discounted and confused are just some of the feelings experienced by a child who needs help. These feelings may erupt in violent explosions at the surface or remain simmering below poised to boil at any moment, but either way are a huge part of the picture. Pictures tell us stories that have a depth beyond objective information. Pictures make it more personal and real. For example, pictures can capture the subtle nuances of a parent's anguish and desperation while watching a child slowly fade away. Examining why, when or how to effectively intervene without acknowledging feelings would be like trying to paint a picture without color; the content within the frame might be familiar, but it lacks depth, contrast and soul. It does not quite resonate to the same degree.

## Sometimes a Coin has Three Sides

Below is a story as told by a teacher, a student and a mother. The student's name is Louis and his mother is Rachel. Our teacher chose to remain anonymous. Let us listen as they tell their story.

### *Teacher's Story*

*I really don't have much to say. I teach Science and am four years from retirement. This is my twenty-first year teaching. It's almost my worst. Between all the ridiculous paperwork and kids like Louis, every day I have to remind myself it is only four more years.*

*Louis doesn't seem to care; he comes to class, sits at his desk and hardly gives an effort. He could make good grades if he wanted to. Louis is a bright kid. But he doesn't turn in homework very often and interrupts class all the time. I am tired of getting on him. I bet I've referred Louis to the office five times this year for mouthing off. He not only is disrespectful, but he makes it difficult for my other students. I have made the request, but they won't transfer him to another teacher. I'm stuck! He just needs to buckle up, get a new attitude and adjust his behavior. When I was a student, this kind of behavior and attitude would result in "the board of education". A few smacks did wonders.*

### *Mother's Story*

*"My name is Rachel and I want to tell you about my son, Louis. Louis is the second of three children and the only boy. My children's father hasn't been involved for years in their lives. As the primary and only parent it all falls on my shoulders to raise them safely. When young, Louis was a joy. When very young, he would come running to the door when his father came home from work, careening into him and wrap both arms around his father's legs. He loved to sit on my lap and be held, rocked, tickled or kissed. In elementary school, he was happy most of the time, made friends easily in the neighborhood, showed interest in youth sports and enjoyed spending time with the rest of us. His grades never gave me reason to worry.*

*In fifth grade, Louis was involved with anti-drug classes along with the rest of his classmates and regularly came home with evidence of his commitment to not use. His school made a strong effort to educate him about the dangers of drinking and drugging and even the local police department did their part in prevention. But, while Louis was learning about what not to do, his father dropped a ton of bricks right on my head by informing me that he no longer loved me, had met someone special and was leaving. Apparently, he had never learned what not to do when it came to marriage. The most accurate word that I know that best describes how his leaving affected my children and me was "devastated". For six months, I cried nightly, pulled away from everyone and tried to make sense of it all, which I never did. During that time, none of my children were given the opportunity to work through their shock, confusion and brokenness. Looking back of course, I feel remorseful, guilty and ashamed about not being there when my kids needed me most. I say that in hindsight. At that time, I was hardly able to get out of bed. He broke my heart and stole my dream of growing old together.*

*Somewhere between seventh and eight grade, I began to see a change with Louis that I assumed was typical teenage angst and rebellion. He began to disengage from the family, preferring to be with friends I did not know well and they were secretive and suspicious acting. Louis began to treat me disrespectfully, as if I was stupid. As a child, he was always sweet and respectful to me. I assumed all of these changes were part of puberty and normal growth. In addition to the change in friends and behavior, school started to suffer. For the first time, Louis' behavior in school was getting him in big trouble.*

*In grade school, he wasn't a perfect angel, but it was nothing like what he started to do later. By the eighth grade, Louis was skipping school, talking back to some of his teachers, bringing home poor grades and seeming not to care. I saw it happening, but was able to do nothing about it. That is when I began to lose my mind with worry. He'd shut down when I tried to talk, walk away when I pressed the issue and on a couple of occasions, said things to me that my father would have killed me for saying to him. There's no need repeating the exact words; we have heard them all. I'd confront him and he'd walk away. I was losing him and did not know what to do. I called his school counselor and was told someone would look into it. I never heard back. I visited our pastor and was told to pray harder. He even suggested that a stronger faith and better attendance at church would help. I walked out feeling ashamed and guilty for not being good enough of a parent. I won't mention what I now think of that man. He was wrong and only made things worse, much worse. I'm not convinced every man of God is a man of God. For awhile, it shook my faith. I regret that now.*

*Things continued to decline in Louis' life. School has become less and less important and he spends a great deal of time with other kids I don't know and don't like. He ignores my questions and stays out as late as he wants. I've lost fifteen pounds and aged fifteen years. Report cards are bad; I don't even want to look. Phone calls from school are horrible; I don't want to answer the phone.*

*I don't talk to my friends, my sister or anyone about our family. I am so angry with Louis that I have thoughts at times no mother should. It all started when my husband abandoned his family. I will not cuss; just know that if I ran into him at the grocery store, security would probably be called. If he had stayed like he promised, none of this would have happened. Our family would still be complete and Louis would be doing much better.*

## Louis' Story

*Some of this happened a long time ago, so I don't remember everything. I know when I was a little kid our family was great. I remember things like Christmas and summer vacations at the beach. We laughed a lot in our home. I remember my dad tickling me until I almost wet my pants laughing. We used to wrestle with dad on his bed. He acted like I had super-human strength and let me win. It was so cool; I flipped, dove and bounced right on top of him. I also remember my mom and dad dancing in the living room to music, with her smiling like it was the happiest day ever. I miss that smile.*

*I don't know all the details, but one day while in sixth grade my dad left for another woman. One day he called us into the living room and announced he was leaving. I should have known something was up because mom was sitting with her head down, crying pretty hard. After that day, I saw my mom fall apart. She cried every night, sometimes she didn't come out of her room and we had to fix our own dinner for a little while. What cut me bad was dad and his new family moved away, he just sort of faded away. I wondered if mom had done something to make him leave. I wondered if I'd done something. I really thought everything was normal up to the day he left home.*

*Mom hardly ever smiled. You know how you can look at someone's eyes and see a hollowed and empty stare? I smoked weed for the first time the summer between sixth and seventh grade with my best friend, Richard, and a new guy from my neighborhood. By the time summer was up, I was getting high almost every day. Being stoned was a whole lot better than not. My mom tried to make me stop, but what could she really do? She couldn't make my dad happy, so why should she be able to make me stop? Richard had it different. His mother put her foot down and grounded him for a month when she found weed in his bedroom. He stopped getting high, but was still my best friend. Well, almost; I really had two best friends, Richard and the new guy Steve.*

*Today school sucks! I hate going and hate my teachers. All they do is write me up because of my "bad attitude". I am mad all of the time, except when stoned. I am barely passing and feel like a permanent member of Saturday D-hall. I definitely get high before that. I don't see Richard much at all. It isn't too bad; I have Steve to hang out with after school.*

*Mom's mad, my home life sucks, school is the pits and my teachers pick on me all the time. But, you know, that's cool because I really don't care about any of that crap anyway!*

If only we possessed a crystal ball and knew everything there was about a kid. Considering everything, it isn't a surprise Louis is struggling. No wonder mom is frustrated. It makes sense. We can even understand why his teacher is so tired and frustrated.

Emotional distress comes in many forms, and exists for many reasons. Acting out behavior is inexcusable, but doesn't "just happen". It is usually because of some factor. There is a reason for what we see. Understanding these reasons and having insight into why students push the limits is invaluable for those of us who need to intervene. It is the closest thing to a crystal ball I know of.

*"The joy of learning is as indispensable in study as breathing is in running. Where it is lacking there are no real students, but only poor caricatures of apprentices who, at the end of their apprenticeship, will not even have a trade."*
**Simone Weil**

# Chapter 3

# Free Attention

Can learning occur in the middle of a catastrophe? How teachable is a student who just learned that a parent has been diagnosed with cancer? What about the child who sits in class preoccupied with who he or she will get (or have) to live with after the divorce is final? In any class, from kindergarten to twelfth grade, a segment of the student population will come through the front doors of our schools, walk into class and sit down in a whirlwind of emotional pain. On the surface, it might not be evident; some students are masterful at hiding that which is most hurtful. Rarely does a child approach a teacher and announce that he or she is not very teachable today because of illness, divorce, death or profound fear. Yet, every day in every school, students struggling with emotional distress experience poor concentration, diminished memory, lowered grades and changed behavior. Though schools do not possess the capability to keep trauma from happening, we know that it is possible to succeed in the classroom even when trauma has occurred. However, this success doesn't happen by accident; *free attention* must be restored. Our ability to successfully perceive and process new information can be referred to as *free attention*. When available, our *free attention* allows us to multi-task, recall information, process data and focus cognitively. But what happens when we temporarily lose our *free attention?*

There appears to be an average of five bits of separate information that can be maintained at one time. These five bits are synonymous with perceiving and processing new information. Under normal conditions, this *free attention* is available for classroom learning, social interaction, working, and playing. When emotionally overwhelmed, students may have most of their *free attention* reduced by issues such as family struggles, peer conflict, chemical dependency, emotional pain, loss, death or disaster, leaving very little capacity to learn in the classroom. Moreover, what little is left is often then reduced because of preoccupation with doing poorly in school.

*Free attention* is analogous to a tabletop. When this table is uncluttered, there is room to put things and rearrange and/or remove items that don't need to be there. However, when the table becomes cluttered, it is difficult to find room for more things, no matter how important. When *free attention* is lost, it is as if our table is too full for new information. Try as one might, there just doesn't seem to be room for perceiving and processing new information.

It's been found that *free attention* is reduced, not so much by a specific incident, but by the emotional trauma that results. In other words, it appears that unresolved feelings reduce *free attention* rather than the actual incident. At some point, all students and adults will temporarily lose *free attention*. Being hungry, physically uncomfortable, worried about a family member, or even having a hole in a sock can reduce *free attention* to some degree. In many cases, with effort, students can restore what is lost by being aware and making an effort to concentrate. However, when the issues reducing *free attention* are severe, the ability to self-restore tends to diminish. The feelings caused by these issues may include sadness, grief, loneliness, worthlessness, shame, hopelessness, helplessness, anger, rage, fear, embarrassment, and terror. It takes effort to deal with feelings and stuffing them takes energy. The loss of *free attention* is due to being overwhelmed by feelings caused by problems that overshadow learning. We can hope this loss is temporary, but these issues can saturate a student's entire school career if unresolved. Suppressed or unresolved feelings are the primary reason for *free attention* being reduced. Healing these hurts or providing emotional support strongly suggests that *free attention* can be restored, thus allowing students to be able to access or utilize their cognitive abilities.

**Free Attention can be Reduced by any of the Following:**

| | |
|---|---|
| Chemical Dependency | Physical Abuse |
| Harmful Involvement | Mental Illness |
| Divorce | Chronic Illness |
| Racial Prejudice | Eating Disorders |
| Sexual Abuse | Death |
| Loss and grief | Chronic Hunger |
| Peer Conflicts | Rage |
| Violence | Severe Poverty |
| Target of Bullying | Extreme Wealth |
| Gender Confusion | Neglect |

The bad news is that schools often can not prevent the above from occurring in a student's life; the good news is schools can reduce the impact of trauma and restore *free attention.*

The *free attention* wheel that follows is an example of a student's life situations and resulting reduction of *free attention.* The pie chart serves to show the number of "bits" of *free attention* a student might possess after experiencing trauma. Circling around this wheel are samples of what problems occur in a student's life. As a consequence, very little *free attention* may be left for the student, often resulting in a drop in grades and changed behavior. This loss then may result in the last bit of *free attention* being captured by feelings of inadequacy, incompetence, and ignorance. Because cognitive functioning is reduced by the lack of *free attention*, those feelings that are most often associated with failure emerge. Without help in restoring the *free attention*, little academic proficiency can be expected.

Whether a researched fact or a metaphor, the *free attention model* does well to demonstrate that when trauma has occurred, expecting a student to "just try harder" or "buckle down and pay attention" has severe limitations. Instead, providing a vehicle for the student to deal with the emotional pain, such as safe and supportive schools, gives the student an opportunity to access his or her cognitive abilities. As we examine other issues often impacting our youth, we will see that this reduction in *free attention* is apparent regardless of whether we are looking at addiction, divorce, abuse, distress, neglect or illness.

### Student:
"I try and I try, but no matter how hard I concentrate it just doesn't sink in. I can't pay attention and I'm forgetting everything. I'm stupid and schools sucks."

### Teacher:
"Just try harder. All you need to do is quit daydreaming. You may be stupid but this class does not suck!"

## Free Attention Wheel

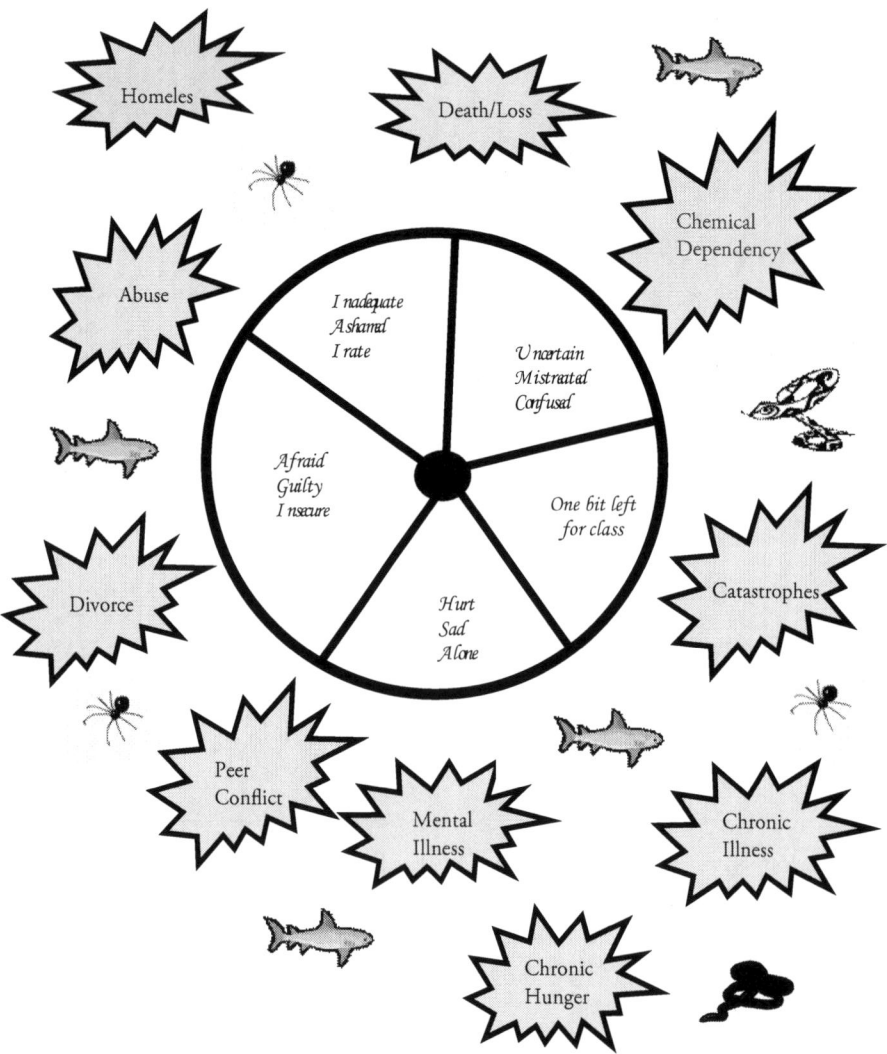

## Restoring Free Attention

Fortunately, it doesn't seem essential to eliminate the outside factors that interfere with *free attention* in order to restore it. The essential thing is to provide a way for the emotional pain to be reduced. Certain types of intervention are an ideal format for offering students the help to increase *free attention*. This is particularly enlightening when we realize help can be accomplished without attempting to resolve the problem. Again, it is not necessary to fix all ills a child has; it helps to provide a way to enhance the student's resilience and success in school. Even under the best of circumstances, it is unreasonable to expect for all five bits to be restored. We all harbor unresolved emotions that take some effort to suppress.

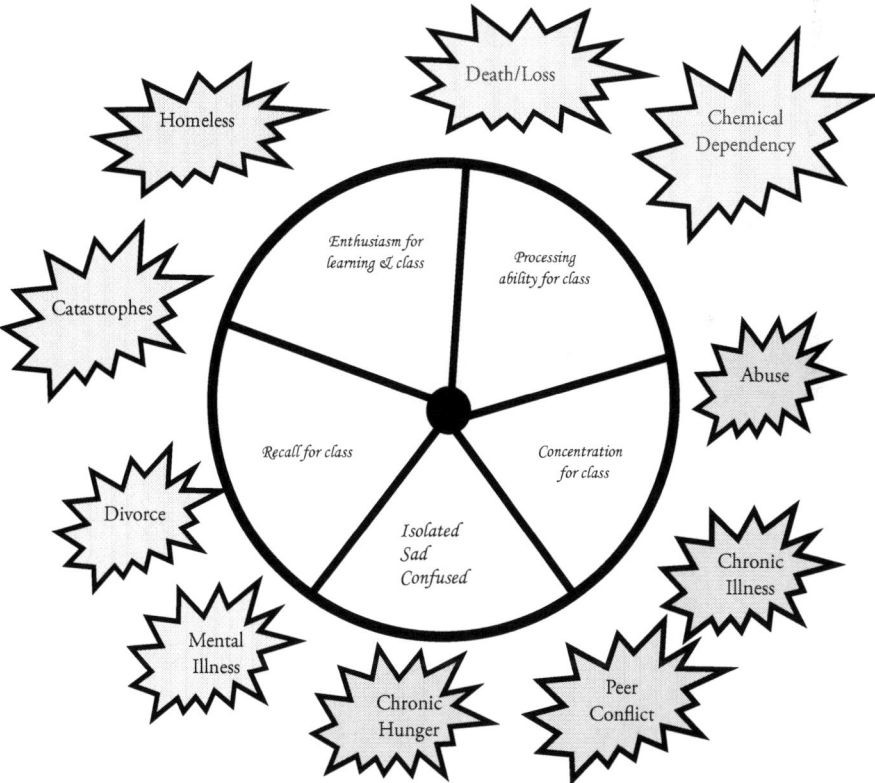

The problems that sometimes hover around our kids cannot be resolved in school. But, in most cases the school can reduce the impact enough for kids to learn. Since it is the feelings that tend to interfere, logic would suggest looking at ways to help the students deal with them. This wheel is a way to illustrate how problems don't go away, but the feelings can be addressed.

In the following example, we can see how a classroom teacher restored the *free attention* of one of her students. It took less than two minutes. You know this kid; he's in every school, in almost every grade. He's angry, defiant, impulsive, loud, abrupt, challenging, offensive, oppositional and a disruption in the classroom. His teacher's ability to teach and her students' ability to learn is challenged and hampered. Realizing that Curt will not respond to requests to take a seat and do his reading assignment, Anna does the following.

## Curt is Hurt

"Curt, could you step out into the hallway with me for a minute?" Reluctantly, he agrees. He figures he can engage his teacher in a power struggle when one-on-one. Away from the ears of other students, the dialogue begins: "It seems you are having trouble in my classroom today." Are you okay"? She asks. Curt responds with anger; "your classroom sucks and you are stupid!" Showing no response to Curt's jab, in a soft tone Anna says; "Well, considering how strongly you feel about my class I'm impressed you showed up."

This isn't the kind of reaction he is used to getting from other adults in his life. Normally Curt engages in a power struggle and wins regardless of the outcome. This time he can't; Anna offers a response that is devoid of having to be powerful. She continues, "It seems today something is troubling you more than on other days. Is there anything going on?" In his typically confrontational manner, Curt answers her with sarcasm; "Just a little bit—considering my dad is going to prison for life and I'll never live with him again." While making this statement, there is a subtle shift in Curt's affect. His sarcasm tapers off and is replaced by what appears to be sadness and discouragement.

Worth noting is Anna's way of responding to Curt's announcement. She says nothing. She doesn't offer condolences or sympathy. She doesn't ask any questions, nor does she try and tell him how he must feel. Anna allows Curt to express his own feelings. His eyes well up and his chin begins to quiver. He won't even blink because doing so would cause the tears in his eyes to roll down his face. That would be crying and he is much too tough to let that happen; after all crying is for emotional girls and weak boys. Within a minute, Curt wipes his eyes with his sleeve, looks at the floor and sighs. As he does this, he tries to push the sadness down. It appears to work, at least on the surface.

Anna breaks her silence with the following: "Curt, considering what you just told me, I want to give you a choice; you can come back to class and do your reading assignment or if desired, I'll let you speak with your counselor. Which would you like to do?" Curt looks at her and says with restored bravado, "I don't care!" Anna does not respond. Instead, she suggests they go back in and see what happens. For the rest of the class period, Curt not only sits down but reads his lesson without interruption. For a moment, Curt's free attention is back. The situation hasn't changed; dad is still going to prison. Yet, after the short interaction, Curt is able to do what he would not (or could not) do prior to the interaction.

## What did Anna do?

1. Removed him from his peers where he would tend to perform.
2. Avoided taking his attitude and words personally. She knows it is not about her.
3. Recognized and validated his efforts, no matter how slight they might have been.
4. Accepted his feelings by remaining quiet. She did not talk him out of his feelings.
5. Acknowledged that what was said was a big deal.
6. Gave him options.
7. Chose to believe he could come back to class and do well.
8. Did not try and change how he felt, or confront the behavior, and lastly she did not make assumptions.

Before the term *free attention* was ever coined, teachers were restoring it. Some did it with specific skills and methods, while others with personality. Regardless of how it is done, the important thing is that it helps the student become teachable again, some temporarily and some for an extended time. I do not think any of us can claim to have remained teachable one hundred percent of the time. *Free attention* comes and goes, it waxes and wanes like the tide. Sadly, for some students once that tide has receded, it does not come back. Boats become grounded, fish die and an offensive stink permeates the air.

So, what does *free attention* have to do with intervention, you ask? For some, the answer may be self-evident and need no explaining. You understand the connection between cognition, emotions and behavior. But, I have learned through years of training adults that the playing field is not level and we do not all read off the same page. We perceive and process information differently. Not only that, but who is to say that as a reader you aren't dealing with your own loss of *free attention*?

In this book, intervention refers to interrupting or redirecting behavior. Behavior is quite often linked to negative feelings (whether the kid knows it or not), and attempts to deal with these feelings often result in a loss of *free attention*. Effective interruptions give students the chance to re-engage in the learning process. Not all respond as hoped, but in my opinion, the majority of young people who act out have not lost that desire deep inside to succeed and be well thought of. Without intervention, the cycle continues, patterns emerge and expectations collapse. A kid's thoughts might sound something like this, *"Because I act bad, I must be bad, and because I am bad, I continue to act bad, which proves that I am bad. What is the point of trying?"*

# Chapter 4

## Distress Patterns

### *Forging a Shield and Sword*

The term *distress pattern* refers to learned behaviors and attitudes developed and utilized by individuals as protection against chronic emotional pain. These patterns are established early in life and appear to initially work very well. Even routine and expected emotional pain tend to stimulate the development of *distress patterns*. In other words, it doesn't take severe trauma; these patterns are a normal part of our development. As the emotional pain (distress) occurs, the unconscious choice is to feel the pain or avoid it. The skills developed to avoid these feelings occur naturally and without much intent. A child who grows up being chronically ridiculed by a parent or peers may begin to act sarcastic or uncaring in order to ward off feelings of inadequacy and insecurity. What starts as a defense mechanism eventually becomes an automatic response that is triggered when something happens that even loosely approximates the original emotional pain. A less traumatic situation such as experiencing the ongoing teasing by an older sibling, enduring the intimidation of starting school, going to the baby sitter, or encountering new situations can give cause for *distress patterns*. They do not necessarily indicate a problem, but possibly more a reaction to life's little "slings and arrows".

Regardless of why they were developed, *distress patterns* begin to lose effectiveness as children get older. Though the perceived protection that these patterns may have provided no longer work as well, they continue to be compulsively used just the same. They become habits or automatic responses to certain incidences. With time, the *distress patterns* not only prove less effective, but actually contribute to the distress by causing more problems. Behaviors or attitudes that worked as protection when young tend to lose their efficacy when older. For example, pouting may work as a *distress pattern* for a young child, but this pattern loses its ability as we get older. Certain behaviors simply are not tolerated by others as we mature.

Incidences of acting out at school can be *distress patterns* that stem from unresolved past emotional hurts. Often students are unable to recall the original hurt and have little insight regarding their behavior. Any situation loosely resembling the original hurt may trigger or re-stimulate the *distress patterns*. The greater the original hurt, the less the approximation needs to be to cause re-stimulation and compulsive responses. Some examples of *distress patterns* may include patterns of *arrogance, apathy, anger, rage, blaming, fragility, non-responsiveness, defiance, resistance, gallows humor, and isolation.*

It is important to remember that not all acting out is a *distress pattern.* Sometimes acting out is testing limits, seeking attention, or evidence of boredom. A key to telling the difference is that students who are testing limits, seeking attention or experiencing boredom tend to respond to redirection or well planned consequences. Students who are displaying *distress patterns* are less likely to redirect their own behavior because they are unaware of why they are acting a certain way. Regardless of the consequences, the acting out continues because of the re-stimulation of feelings. This in no way excuses a student from being accountable for his or her behavior, but it does give reason as to why we see some students engage in a self-defeating behavior, even when this should be apparent to him or her.

Distress patterns develop in sometimes very subtle ways, often without thought. The following series of entries document how distress patterns can be triggered in just about anyone, including you . . . Follow the progression!

## We Start Young

### Age Five

It is a beautiful Saturday morning and you are just finishing a bowl of Captain Crunch and watching your favorite cartoons. Your daddy calls you to the garage and tells you he has a very special job for you. He really needs your help. How fun to be helping daddy with a real job. Daddy is a really super guy and takes the time to give you easy jobs that you can do; while he does the hard ones. You are only five years old. After a whole hour of working, with daddy drinking his iced tea and you drinking your Sunny Delight, he announces that because of your super good work, the job is almost done. Daddy says that the last thing to do is to sweep up the big pile on the floor that is in the middle of the garage. It is a mixture of sawdust, dirt, dog hair, dead insects, dryer lint and cobwebs. It's pretty big. It's pretty gross, too. Your daddy tells you to hold the dustpan steady so he can sweep the mess up with his push broom. You bend down carefully so as not to touch the dead insects. Cobwebs are nasty and you are careful to not to let them touch you. Yuck! And dead bugs are even worse! Just as he begins to sweep, his cell phone rings and he answers it. You notice a frown on his face; he was smiling before the call.

He covers the mouthpiece and tells you he has to go inside for about five minutes and for you to keep up the good work. He gives a thumbs-up and gives you that wink that always makes you laugh. He goes inside. You are feeling happy and lucky, standing with a dustpan in hand and a big pile of stuff that needs to be swept up. Daddy said you were a great little worker, didn't he. Well, you get a great idea. What if you cleaned the rest all by yourself? Even with cobwebs and dead bugs, you are planning to sweep every single bit of the gross stuff up. You place the dustpan on the ground, so the pile will go in when you sweep. You grab the push broom and begin. Something is not working. You push the broom and the dustpan slides back. The pile doesn't go in. The more you try, the messier it gets. Even though you are five-years-old-going-on-six, you are distracted and the broom turns into a big paintbrush. You start painting. Then it turns into an airplane and you fly around the garage floor making airplane noises. Then your broom becomes a car driving on a twisting, winding road. You are having so much fun you've forgotten the job you were trying to do. After all, you are only five-going-on-six.

Daddy comes out; he's off the phone and he's upset. You are confused because you thought he was happy doing this job with you. He sees what you've done. He turns toward you, with a scary look and in a loud unfriendly voice says, "I can't even leave you alone for five minutes without you messing things up. Can't you do anything right?" You notice outside the garage that dark storm clouds are rolling in. Way off in the distance you hear thunder; something has changed.

Before you can answer, he tells you to get inside and that he would have to do everything over again. You are confused! Five minutes ago you were a great little worker, helping your daddy do a job. Everyone was happy. Now he says you can't do anything right. This breaks your little heart. You drop your head, drop your shoulders and sadly go inside. You sit down and start to cry, but not too loud. You don't want mommy to know because then she won't be happy.

How do you feel? At your age you don't know the words to describe it. If you did, you'd say you felt stunned, crushed, devastated, inadequate, insignificant, stupid and guilty. You also feel shame and you do not know how this is different from guilt. Do you feel loved right now? What in the world is wrong with you? It breaks your heart and you silently sit and cry until you begin to tell yourself that cleaning the garage is dumb. Daddy can clean it by himself next time. You don't care if it is dirty and full of dead bugs. You didn't want to really clean it anyway. It can stay dirty forever and ever. Right now, you just don't care. You turn the TV back on and watch some dumb old show where that dad is never mean.

After an hour, your daddy sits down next to you. He tries to make small talk, but you don't look at him; you are still upset. He turns, gently lifts your chin so you can look at his eyes. Now he is not mad, instead he looks very sad. Your daddy tells you how sorry he is for being so mean. He explains he was really angry about the phone call. He says he didn't mean any of what he said and that he loves you more than anything in the world. You quietly ask him as if you aren't sure, "all the way to the moon daddy?" Now his eyes look even sadder and you see him wipe his face with his sleeve. "To the moon and back again, sweetheart" he says. He asks if you will forgive him. You answer by hugging his neck (you always liked how dad smelled). He wants you to know why he acted like such a jerk and asks if you would go with him to get ice cream and talk. You smile, nod and take hold of his hand.

## Kindergarten

It is a couple of months later and you are in kindergarten. You are now six years old. Your teacher is Miss Sharp and she's real nice. There are about twenty other kids in class with you. You like school and look forward to getting to do new stuff. Miss Sharp reads a story every day. You get to make things and even learn letters like big kids. You almost know your ABC's. Today Miss Sharp held up a note, asking if someone would do her a favor. She needs someone to take a piece of paper down to the office. Almost every hand goes up and your hand is one of the very first. You are jumping in your seat with excitement. Miss Sharp looks up from her desk and calls out a name without even looking around. She picks Shelly again. Shelly is picked for everything. Disappointed, you put your arm down and fold both in front of you. You are no longer bouncing in your seat. Miss Sharp didn't even notice you. It makes you mad; it's unfair. With a frown on your six year-old face, you utter under your breath, "I didn't want to take that stupid note to the office anyway. So, what if she always picks Shelly. They are both dummies." You tell yourself that you really don't care.

## Fourth Grade

Today you hate school worse than anything. Your grades are okay, but you are not very good at sports. You try, but almost every kid in class can run faster. Who cares anyway so you don't even try your hardest, though you used to. Today in physical education, your class was split into two teams to play kick ball. The two fastest kids are once again made captains and pick a number between one and ten to see who goes first. Here it goes again; it's like all the other times. It's always the same ones picked first, the popular and cool kids. You don't even get your hopes up. Instead of trying to be noticed, you begin to work yourself to the back of the room so you aren't seen. It doesn't matter; you will be one of the last picked anyway. You don't make eye contact or look interested in playing on a team. It's down to the last four picks and you no longer can hide. You see the captain of the team look at you, move on and then pick someone else. Finally, there is no one left but you. You really do hate school at this moment.

You are embarrassed and won't look up. The captain with the last pick looks at the coach and asks aloud; "Do we have to? It won't help anyway." The coach doesn't even say anything about what was just said. It is like you don't count. Some kids even laugh. The words cut deep, but you don't show it. Instead, you put your hands in your pockets and with an "I don't care about any of this" expression; you walk over to the team. You aren't wanted on this team and feel yourself turning red. You feel small and unimportant. You feel rejected. This is why you hate school.

You want desperately to be like all the other kids. You want to fit in, be a part of the team, and to be picked any other position than last. That may be what you wish, but your words and actions scream aloud the exact opposite. Your classmates see that you aren't interested and could care less. At least they think that. They don't realize your apathy is driven by the rejection, but then again neither do you. Not only do you feel less important than others, but others see you as less important. In your awkward attempts to protect yourself from the bad feelings, you make things even worse. How totally disappointing! All you do is remind yourself that you really don't care. Who wants to be picked first anyway? It doesn't mean anything. You ignore what others say about you and act invisible. To yourself, you constantly whisper, "Who cares anyway?"

## Eighth Grade

American history is almost over. School is different now. You have lost that "baby fat" and have grown four inches taller since last year. You no longer are picked last and you actually are pretty good at sports. You were even invited to a party a couple of weekends ago. Other people see you differently than they did in elementary school. In your head, that little voice keeps telling you that you are the same dorky and awkward kid who was so unpopular. What is hard for you to believe is that people don't see you that way. It's like you are one of the cool kids, but you still don't believe it. Slowly your self-image is changing, but it is changing on the inside much slower that the outside. It will take a while before you actually believe the nice things others say. In the meantime, you keep waiting for people to learn the truth and once again pick you last.

All period long, you've been sneaking peaks at another student that you have a great big crush on. The first time you see this person, something special happens. You start to think about this person even when you aren't in class. Just looking at her makes your palms sweat and heart pound. When you talk to her, you are tongue-tied. But, you can't help but smile. Today, she smiled back. Her smile told you that maybe, just maybe, she might even like you. Unbelievable! When you walk down the halls, your feet feel two inches above the floor and your head is in the clouds. These are happy days and the sun is shining.

This afternoon, there is a home game right after school and most of the students attend, including your secret heartthrob. You've seen this person at the game several times before hanging out with friends, laughing and having a good time. Today is the big day. You decide you are going to invite her to sit with you at the game and maybe even walk over there together. As scared as you are, you tell yourself not to back down. The bell rings and class is over. You've worked up enough courage to walk right up to her and ask, "Would you go with me to the game after school?" You have practiced these words over and over in your head. You've chickened out two times already and this has to be different. You take a deep breath and steel yourself.

As you begin walking over, you see another person get there first. You frown, hesitate and stand back. The two of them are in engaging in a conversation that you cannot hear, but you figure this person has asked first and for you it is too late now. Without following through with your plan, you give up. Discouraged and very disappointed, you walk by the two of them hoping for a smile or something that would restore your confidence. You are not even noticed! They are too busy looking at something. You decide to just go home.

Unknown to you, they were only discussing a homework assignment. That's it! As a matter of fact, after you've left, the target of your affection looked around hoping to say "hi" before you got away. After all, you smiled back. While walking alone your thoughts formulate to ease the disappointment. You've felt this way plenty of times before. This is a familiar feeling, even though the situation is new. "I didn't really want to go with her anyway", you think to yourself. You add, "I was stupid for ever hoping I had a chance. I really didn't want to go to the game that badly". A familiar thought echoes through your head, "who really cares anyway?" You place your hopes and desires into that same secret box you have placed other disappointments. This box is hidden deep in the pit of your stomach where it stays locked, private and alone. Sometimes you don't care about anything.

## Eleventh Grade

It has happened in the families of many of your friends, so what's the big deal, you ask yourself. Plus, you are almost grown and on your own. Just a couple of more years and you'll be off to college. Being able to afford college is unlikely. A lot of things are unlikely now. Two nights ago, your mom came to your bedroom and said she needed to talk. You were sitting at your desk, listening to music, and you told her to come in. Putting the earphones down, you turned to see what she wanted. You have always gotten along with your mom, even in the last couple of years when a lot of kids can't stand their parents. In your case, it is just your dad you cannot tolerate. Your mom tells you through teary eyes and a constricted voice that your father has informed her that he has fallen in love with another woman. You learn he has already moved out that day and will come back later to get the rest of his stuff. It is obvious to you that your mom's heart is breaking. You notice her hands trembling; she has dark circles under both eyes, and she acts as if someone has just died. She's barely hanging on. All you can think about is what a loser your father is.

This news hits you right in the gut. You find in the next few days there are no words that can really capture what has happened. You also notice that for the next couple of months, there is very little talk at home and definitely no laughter. "Glum" and "dark' are words that best describe your home now. Below the surface, you feel a growing sense of discouragement. However, on the surface you look strong. All of your energy is going towards your mom; she's the one who needs support right now. Things are backwards now. Instead of you being cared for, you are taking care of her. You do not mind doing this at all. She is devastated and not in the parenting role now. Listless and depressed, mom lost the spark that made her so special. The woman your dad fell in love with and promised to love forever is no longer present. At night, you hear her crying and you don't know what to do. You stand at her door poised to knock, but walk away out of fear you'll embarrass her. When your dad comes to get his things, you can't speak to him or even look at him. You don't want to cry in front of him. You don't want him to know how horrible you think he is. In addition, if you start to talk, the anger, resentment and rage will erupt like Mount St. Helens. The damage would be immeasurable. So, you just stare at him when he walks by. He tries to talk to you but there is no way you will listen. He can go talk to his new girlfriend, for all you care.

Over the next couple of days, you put a lot of effort into stuffing your feelings. At school, you notice that you are not really paying attention. You are there physically, but not mentally. Your body shows up, but your heart and soul stay at home. You walk the school hallways with a worried scowl on your face. For you, even when it is bright and shiny outside, it is dark and gloomy inside. Darkness now is a time of emptiness, worry, fear and anger. Twice you are confronted by teachers because you are not paying attention. You don't turn homework in because you don't do it. You just failed a major science test, once one of your favorite classes. So what! As far you are concerned, you just don't care.

Your family is falling apart and school is a big zero; you don't have a friend to talk to and your mom is slowly fading away right in front of you. You fail three more tests in the next couple of weeks and find that you don't care one way or another. What is the point of planning for the future when the present is hardly worth living? You don't know it, but underneath all of the miserable feelings boiling inside you about your dad is one more thought; you feel like a failure. Nothing is working at home, at school and your friendships reek. You just give up like a sinking ship spinning down a whirlpool. There is nothing to be done; you feel helpless.

Your counselor calls you into her office and says something about your drop in grades and unusual behavior. She wants to know if everything is okay. You just shrug, tell her a lie, and walk out mumbling something like "what's the point anyway?" Anger now hardens you. Others notice you seem irritated all the time and people avoid you more than usual. Teachers are perplexed by how unapproachable you are. Somehow, others know to stay out of your way. You have a short fuse and can go off at any point. One teacher, Mrs. Landry, who used to be your favorite, asks you to stay after class. You kind of know why and are resolved to just sit at your desk and not talk. She says, "Until the last couple of weeks, you have been a hard worker in class, seeming to care about your work. You were doing well, so I know you can, but right now, you are not doing very well. What's going on?" Her kindness hits you in the one soft spot you have left and you tear up. The lump in your throat almost hurts because it is so big. You want to tell her what the deal is. You need to tell her before you turn to stone and sink away. You open your mouth to express the turmoil and catastrophe that your life is now and you hear the following words come out of your mouth: "It doesn't matter! No one can fix it, no one can help." You look up at her and continue; "It's really not a big deal, plenty of others have it worse. Plus, what does it matter?" Mrs. Landry tries to say something, but you cut her off by walking out. As you leave her class, you look back and say, "Everyone can just get off my back; I really don't care anymore." You wrap this attitude around you like a parka on a cold winter's night. It might be frigid, but it doesn't bother you one bit. Moreover, if it did, you wouldn't care. After all, you really don't care about anything.

## Early Adulthood

Oh, how you hate starting a new job. Meeting all these people for the first time worries you. You've always dreaded social situations and preferred to be alone. At least that is what you've convinced yourself. On a break, you go to get a Diet Coke out of the machine. As you open the door where the vending machine is, you see five co-workers yet to be introduced sitting together snickering. You see them look up barely containing their laughter. They look guilty of something and you are pretty sure you know exactly why. You just happen to have walked in right as they were most likely talking about you. Whatever was said apparently was funny to them. They just didn't know you were about to walk in and catch them talking about you. They don't even know you and they are making fun of you. You figure it is because you are the new person. They are no better than a bunch of fourth graders, you think. You refuse to make eye contact; walk straight to the vending machine to get your drink and walk out. Not a word is spoken; you don't nod your head, say hello or even glance their way.

The feelings are familiar; unfortunately, they are not new. Rejection, embarrassment, confusion and anger all course through your emotional veins. After you walk out, the five look at each other in a perplexed manner wondering what in the world is wrong with you. They had been talking about the principal's new hairpiece, and how awful it looked. They were embarrassed when you walked in because they thought you overheard them laughing, being snide and insensitive. Ignoring them confirmed their concern. As you leave the break room, you make a vow to avoid people and just keep to yourself. You were overheard saying, "I don't need to put up with this. I don't want to even be in the same room with them." While walking back to your office you remind yourself that you just don't care anyway. Why would you?

## As The Years Go By

From an early age, you learned a particular way to protect your feelings when you sensed rejection and disapproval. You forged a shield or distress pattern by convincing yourself that you just don't care anyway. You've been this way for as long as you remember. It must be your wiring or DNA. You continued to use this shield when you sensed the rejection coming (re-stimulated distress pattern) and it began to be the problem. By attempting self-protection, you actually achieved the opposite. You learned this distress pattern when you were too young to recall. In kindergarten, this shield wasn't a big deal. In fourth grade, it began to backfire and ostracized you from your classmates. In eighth grade, you walked away from your heart's desire, playing it safe. You were a sailing vessel that wouldn't leave the harbor. You will always regret not taking that risk. After all sailing ships weren't meant to remain in the harbor. That is not why they were made. In eleventh grade, your world falls apart and you have no power to stop it. The only solace is to remember that you really don't care. As an adult, you become anti-social when anything loosely approximates some ancient memory. Your distress patterns worked at one time but became less effective as you got older and harmfully worked against your best interests. But, maybe that doesn't really bother you too much. Maybe you just don't care anymore.

*"Speak when you are angry and you will make the best speech you will ever regret."*
*Ambrose Bierce*

## When Your Buttons Get Pushed

Probably every adult who has worked with young people has had his or her buttons pushed. It seems to come with the territory of working with youth. But, there are those among us who may be more prone to this happening than others. For reasons, some of us take students' comments or behavior much more personal. We get hit in a spot that brings on a strong emotional response. As a educators, there will be times when a student's attitude or words will re-stimulate your distress patterns, challenging you to remain objective and detached. This doesn't mean our reaction should be callous, cold or uncaring, but it does ask us to buffer our emotional reactions when responding to students. It usually isn't about you, but rather something the student is struggling with.

As adults working with kids it is vital to know what your buttons are, or understand your own distress patterns. This self-awareness will contribute tremendously to your own ability to avoid your distress patterns from getting in the way. It is much harder to get blind-sided by a student's comment when you are aware of your buttons.

### Adult distress patterns may result in:

> ➤ Controlling the class excessively
> ➤ Ignoring or freezing a student out
> ➤ Using sarcasm or passive-aggressive comments
> ➤ Wearing feelings on your shoulder—hypersensitive
> ➤ Shaming or blaming a student
> ➤ Snide or smug response to a student
> ➤ Violating boundaries
> ➤ Being condescending and judgmental

## It's Crunch Time

Without opening his mouth, the patient's affect telegraphed anger and hostility. He boasted a skinhead look, displayed vulgarity on one hand, with a curse word permanently tattooed on his left knuckles, and the word *"hate"* permanently inked on his right. His first name was Neil, but he preferred the street name of "Crunch", which seemed to fit. The counseling staff called him "Neil" because the term "Crunch" did not fit into the recovery atmosphere of the inpatient adolescent treatment program he was in. Beyond his appearance, Neil worked hard to alienate himself from staff and other patients. Twice he tossed something out his sixth floor window, his schoolbooks one day and his urine on another day. He blew his nose in a piece of bread and offered it to fellow patients. He refused to interact in group therapy and shut down other patients who wanted to participate. His foul language will not be repeated; we've all heard it before.

With a mounting agreement from the staff, Crunch's doctor wrote an order to transfer him to the third floor Psychiatric Intensive Care Unit (PICU). He would go from a relatively open unit, where patients had the freedom to do things like eat in the cafeteria and hang out in the dayroom, to a place with padded walls and locked doors. I was asked to escort him to the third floor during the transfer. When informed about his transfer, Crunch seemed apathetic and unconcerned. He shrugged and spewed forth more vulgarity.

We got on the elevator on the sixth floor, destination third floor, PICU. At the fifth floor, the door opened and two other hospital employees entered. We continued our descent without incident. That was about to change. Without me noticing, Crunch slowly drew in a deep breath, cleared the phlegm from his throat, gathered a huge wad in his mouth and spit directly on my shirt. Spittle, phlegm and mucous splattered the front of my shirt. My strongest visual memory was seeing his sludge-like expectorant floating in my coffee cup. I almost quit drinking coffee.

Without much rational consideration, I quickly glanced at the two other riders, sized Crunch up and asked the following "therapeutic" question: *"When do you turn eighteen?"* He replied with an insolent, *"Why do you want to know?"* I responded, *"You'll be an adult at that time and not a patient in our treatment center. I'm going to find you and beat the hell out of you for doing this."* The elevator grew awkwardly quiet. The other two riders seemed to freeze without comment or eye contact. They quickly left when the doors opened on the next floor.

Without further comments from either of us, Crunch and I rode the elevator to the third floor. Crunch entered PICU and I did not see or talk with him for the duration of his stay. I was not shunning him; I did not work on the third floor and rarely went there. That evening I told a friend that there was a patient in treatment that was so hard to deal with that if God came to me in a dream with a button that would have made Crunch unborn, I'd have pushed it. My friend gasped, opened his eyes wide with dismay and scoffed at the idea, thinking I was not the type to say such a thing. I thought the same myself. I clarified that what I meant was that it probably would have been better if Crunch had never been born. I saw Crunch as a person with no redeeming value. I appointed myself Crunch's cop, judge, jury and executioner and continued my venting, *"It's like Eva Braun and Adolph Hitler had a child and he's in our hospital. No, a better analogy is that Satan apparently sired a son and his name is Crunch."* Looking back, I still find it hard to believe I became that angry, defensive and arrogant. One thing I "knew" was that Crunch did not have a chance to get sober; he was way too sick, or so I thought.

Six months later, while attending a local 12-step meeting, I saw Crunch. There he was with the same vulgar writings on his knuckles. However, he looked different, but I just couldn't put my finger on it. We made brief eye contact throughout the meeting. When the Serenity Prayer finished and the meeting ended, he walked up to me and inquired, *"Do you remember me?"* In front of me stood the only ex-patient/client that I had ever threatened to beat up; of course I remembered him! I played it cool saying, *"Yeah, it's Crunch, right"?* With what appeared a look of embarrassment, he told me he now went by his given name, "Neil". He then knocked my socks off by continuing, *"I'm six months sober now and working on my eighth and ninth step."* Of the twelve steps, these two have to do with making amends. Looking me straight in the eyes, Neil said with total sincerity, *"I've wanted to tell you how much I regretted what I did to you on the elevator that day. I was wrong and still feel bad about it."*

A tightened throat and a blurred vision hampered my immediate response. His words completely hit me unexpectedly. I don't know what I expected, but it certainly was not this kid making amends. When composed enough to respond, I told him how disappointed I was in what I said as well. I also found myself silently regretting making the arrogant prediction of his failure and lack of inherent worth. Neil and I shared how good it was to be able to make these amends. We had an understanding at that moment that transcends all handshakes, contracts or deeds. Appreciation replaced resentment. Faith pushed out cynicism. Encouragement took the place of negativity. I walked away that day emotionally limping, keenly aware of being humbled. My comments and judgments were proven very wrong. They bounced back at me; ricocheting, sending broken shards of arrogance in all directions.

## Timeless Lessons

1. *Do not give up until after a person's last breath is drawn.*

2. *It is impossible to make a prognosis on how someone will do.*

3. *We all have buttons; regardless of how masterful our skills.*

That night I called my friend and announced, *"Today, I witnessed a miracle!"* Sometimes the best lessons are taught in a much-disguised manner.

## What does this have to do with Distress Patterns?

Many years ago, I owned a letter jacket my grandmother had given me for Christmas. The color was burnt-orange, the same as the University of Texas. As an Austin native, I loved U.T. football. Easily, this jacket was the coolest thing I owned.

After a muddy day playing soccer at P.E., the class-bully walked up and wiped his muddy hands on my jacket with total impunity. In my mind I saw myself pushing and tripping this guy, thrashing away until he apologized. No one was going to disrespect me that way. It wasn't so much that I had been disrespected; it was that the jacket had. In reality I looked down at the mud streaks, turned and walked away afraid, embarrassed, ashamed and humiliated. The sum of those feelings was an intense desire to take up for myself. Because I did not, the self-condemnation overshadowed everything else. Time passed and I forgot the incident. I had no recall what happened to the jacket and did not remember the bully's name.

Little did I know that almost sixteen years later I would make that stand with my own level of impunity. How dare someone spit on me like that. No one was going to spit on me! What did this kid think he was doing? Instead of a sixth grade classroom, it was a hospital elevator. Instead of being twelve years of age, I was twenty-eight. Instead of a bully, it was a patient. This is the power of distress patterns. Knowledge really is power, power to avoid stupid reactions, risky behaviors and arrogant assumptions. Do you know your distress patterns? Are you aware of your buttons? These questions can be rhetorical or literal; it is your choice. My strong suggestion is that you identify those sensitive areas before saying or doing something regrettable.

I lost track of Neil and have no idea of how he's doing or where he is. He has never been too far away from me when it comes to knowing my distress patterns. Unresolved issues do not go away; at best, they lay dormant until the right time comes. Then they emerge in a clumsy, awkward, hurtful and inadequate fashion.

# I am Right Here

I have forgotten who I am
I think I never really knew
My age does not matter
At least not to me

When I look inside
All I see is a hole
Before me the ground broken
Full of shards of glass and thorns

I disappear right before your eyes
Stay away, I do not need you
Keep out of reach to remain secure
Don't listen to me, I am confused

Surely, I am more than nothing
Perhaps vapor in a strong wind
To adult eyes, I am diminishing fog
Still, I am right here

If eyes cannot see me
Nor ears catch a sound
Like fallen trees in a forest
Did I even exist?

This is not what I hoped for
My dreams were like yours
Dreams are just wishes that never come true
Wishes just hopes that crumble

Before I go away, I want one last try
With each kick and each scream I say, "I am here"
It is good that I kick
It is good that I scream

I grasp with sad anger
I reach from within
You will notice me now
Here I go

# Chapter 5

# Learned Hopelessness

*Learned hopelessness* can result from a number of situations. Some kids give up and others fight back. In either case, someone somewhere needs to intervene before it reaches critical mass.

There was a study done where behavioral researchers constructed two identical cages large enough in which a dog could move around. These two cages were then wired with enough electricity to cause a moderate shock on the floor of the cage. The only difference was one cage was shut, while the other was left open. Upon the initial shock, both dogs sought relief, with one dog jumping out of the cage and the other searching for an escape. To no avail, this dog tried what limited resources it had to remedy the situation. It yelped, barked, jumped and alternated how many paws touched the floor at the same time. After repeatedly going through these ineffective efforts, the dog appeared to give up. When shocked, the dog no longer tried to get away. The consequence was that the dog lay down and accepted the shock as something that could not be avoided.

After observing this "giving up" cycle, the researchers opened the door to the cage, and tried to find a way to motivate the dog to jump out, or contradict this sense of hopelessness. To their surprise, when enticed by further shocks, or the offering of food and affection, the dog did not leave the cage. The dog could see an open door, but was unwilling (unable?) to step out. In order to get the dog to leave the cage, the researchers had to manually pull the dog across the threshold more than one hundred times before it re-learned that it had the power to leave the painful situation.

Obviously, children are not dogs in a cage. However, children are often in a situation that is hurtful and when it becomes evident to them that nothing is working and no one is helping to make it better, *learned hopelessness* can set in. We see apathy, depression, self-deprecation, self-cutting, alcohol and other drug use. We see attempts to minimize the sense of hopelessness.

*Learned hopelessness* can occur when a person repeatedly tries to avoid, stop or reduce emotional pain without success. A student's best attempt to deal with the situation is ineffective. This can include dealing with parental addiction, sexual abuse, severe poverty, and being the target of chronic bullying behavior. *Learned hopelessness* can look like giving up—a sense of despair where one just quits trying. Some students choose behaviors that can contradict this hopelessness, such as acting out, bullying others, vandalism, chemical use, defiance, etc.

*Learned hopelessness* may be a form of Post Traumatic Stress Disorder, and more information on PTSD is included in this book. Whether it is or is not, children need to feel a sense of control. They need to be properly empowered whenever possible. Getting opportunities to make decisions is beneficial to young people. As adults in their world, we either contribute to a young person's *learned hopelessness* (by ignoring it) or help contradict it (by responding).

It is difficult to look at a group of children or adolescents and pick out those who are feeling this sense of hopelessness. Kids have many ways of hiding their thoughts and feelings. If adults were trauma-informed, all kids could be treated as if *learned hopelessness* existed. All kids need empowerment, control and a sense of self-direction. With those struggling with learned hopelessness, these characteristics can provide healing. With kids who are not, these characteristics still have tremendous benefits.

## Stainless Steel Chassis

At birth, children are like a stainless steel chassis; perfect, untarnished and full of potential. Throughout the years, this chassis is dented, scraped and dulled. The windshield is cracked and the tailpipe drags the ground. Paint is poorly re-applied and baling wire is used to hold things together. The child forgets he or she was ever a stainless steel chassis and begins to confuse the body on the outside for the essence of who he or she really is.

On the outside, others see a vehicle that appears broken down, full of defects and slowly coming apart. Too many coats of paint have been applied. Colors do not match; scratches can be seen on the hood and stains are bleeding through. The doors do not match, tires are dangerously bald and the antennae is missing. Sadly, the child sees the same thing and assumes that there never was a time when none of these defects existed.

No matter how bad the car looks, no matter how poorly it runs, and no matter how junked, there is a forgotten understanding that needs to be rediscovered. Under all of that paint, stains, scratches, dents and cracks remains the original stainless steel chassis. It is at its core as perfect as the day it came off the assembly line of life. Nothing can take that away. It is God given and something to be deeply cherished.

As adults who work with children, we need to help each one come to understand how he or she really is stainless steel. No matter what others have said, no matter what kind of trauma has been inflicted and no matter what kind of self-talk there is, it does not change a thing. There may need to be repairs to the body, old paint scraped off, and the windshield and tires replaced. There may need to be some major work done or possibly just a touch up and wax job. At no time has the inherent value of the child been diminished. It may take a great deal of effort convincing the child, but once there is a full recognition of how wonderful he or she is on the inside, the more likely the child will believe things can get better.

# What about these Three?

## Rene'—age 15

Rene' heard dad threaten mom with these words; "If you drink one more time or take those damn pills again, I am taking these kids out of your life and you will never, ever see them again." He was not playing around. When dad said things, he meant it. That afternoon Rene' got off the school bus, walked into her house and found mom passed out on the couch. Next to her was a half empty bottle of wine and a new bottle of prescription pain killers with the top off. Looking at the clock, Rene' realizes she has about two hours before dad gets home. In those two hours, she cleans, cooks, gets mom showered and manages to make everything look okay. Dad got home, smelled dinner cooking, observed a clean home, and saw his wife in the kitchen with no evidence of drinking or drugging. It worked! Rene' kept her family together that afternoon. The problem is that every day Rene' will get off the bus and maybe do the same thing. She can't participate in after school activities and won't bring any friends home.

## Terry—age 12

Terry tried many things to keep her uncle from coming into her room at night. She did not bathe for a week, hoping that would somehow make him stay away. She wore three pair of undergarments to bed, again hoping that layering herself with clothes would offer some protection. Both of these strategies failed. In desperation, she shoved her heavy dresser in front of the door, knowing that he was stronger and could easily shove it back. She was trying to give him the message, "Leave me alone!" This did not work either. Finally, one morning Terry asked her mom in a very timid voice, "*Mom, do you think I can get a lock on my door?*" Dismissing her daughter's request, the response was; "*That's silly, Terry. Why would you need that?*" Terry did not answer. Every strategy she tried failed. What else was she to do? Some might ask why she didn't tell somebody. No way! Her cousin said something when the same man was going in her room and the entire family accused her of lying and wanting attention. This accusation seemed to hurt as much as the actual violations. Terry did not want to go through what her poor cousin went through. She'd just keep her mouth shut and hoped it would eventually stop.

## Jason—age 17

Jason didn't understand why he was being beaten up at school all the time. He never did anything to deserve it. He was always quiet, kept to himself and tried not to draw attention. It did not help! What really upset him was that teachers saw him being ganged upon and just turned the other way, as if it was okay with them that he got kicked around. At first, he was hoping someone would step up. There wasn't a safe place in the school for him. He was bullied in the hallway, bathroom, cafeteria, and gymnasium. He was even harassed while walking to school. He tried three different routes to get to school, thinking that he'd find one that was safe. It was like this one group of boys lived to make his life miserable.

Jason talked with his counselor, who said that there was really nothing that could be done. *"Boys will be boys"* was his reply and he stated if every time the school addressed someone being pushed around, there wouldn't be time for class. Jason was told he was just going to have to deal with it himself. The last thing his counselor said was, *"Don't let this bother you."* All Jason could do was stare across the desk before getting out of the chair and walking out. That was the day he realized that there was nothing that would be done. At home, his father just told him to fight back, and if he didn't, he deserved what he got. Then dad made it clear, *"A man's got to stand up for himself in this world. Don't expect me to come running every time you bump your toe."*

Going to school was the worst thing in his life and many times he faked being sick just to avoid the beatings. Jason wrote in his journal last night about finally doing something about it. If no one else would help, he would take things a lot further than anyone imagined. He often fantasized about coming to school with a gun and teaching every single person a lesson. Things couldn't be any worse. As far as he was concerned, life was not worth living anyway.

*"Call it a clan, call it a network, call it a tribe, and call it a family. Whatever you call it, whoever you are, you need one."*
**Jane Howard**

# Chapter 6

## Family Systems

We will look at the family for the primary reason that it plays such a large part in any student's life. Family dynamics influences how we adults interact with kids. Insight about the student is great; insight about you is priceless. This is not an attempt to assign blame or point fingers at anyone. If we were to blame the parents, they in turn could blame their parents, and so on. We are reminded of the teenager in the northeast who sued his parents for poor parenting. The judge threw it out based on the supposition that, if allowed, these parents then could sue their parents (who were deceased) and so on. The judge's *Solomon-like* suggestion to the young man was to stop pointing at what the parents did poorly and make a commitment to do better when he became a parent. Instead of looking for blame, look for answers. Instead of looking back, look forward. When referring to the family, the term system is used to describe how a family operates as a single entity, made up of numerous individuals. Within the system, the following dynamics exist:

> **Nothing exists in a vacuum.**
> **For every action, there is reaction.**
> **All systems strive for balance - status quo.**
> **System members unknowingly adopt survival roles.**
> **Systems operate by an unwritten and unspoken set of rules.**
> **The needs of the system outweighs the needs of the individuals.**

The focus of this section is primarily on dysfunctional family systems. In order to give some relevance to the word dysfunction, the following lists contrast healthy systems with dysfunctional ones:

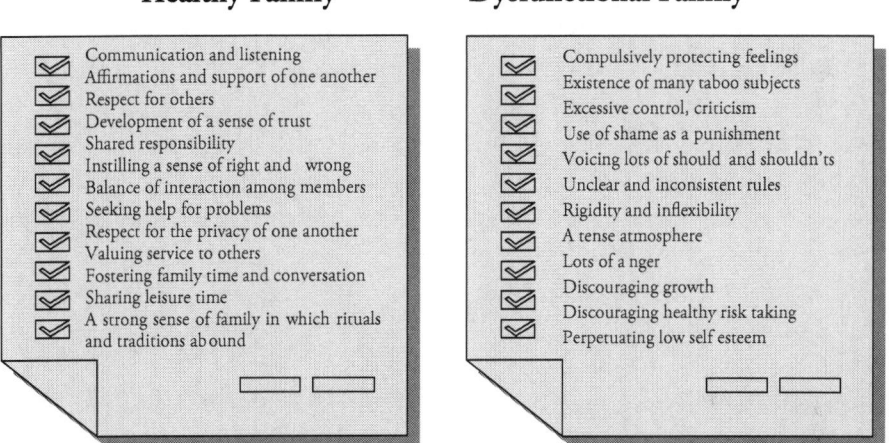

**Healthy Family**

- ☑ Communication and listening
- ☑ Affirmations and support of one another
- ☑ Respect for others
- ☑ Development of a sense of trust
- ☑ Shared responsibility
- ☑ Instilling a sense of right and wrong
- ☑ Balance of interaction among members
- ☑ Seeking help for problems
- ☑ Respect for the privacy of one another
- ☑ Valuing service to others
- ☑ Fostering family time and conversation
- ☑ Sharing leisure time
- ☑ A strong sense of family in which rituals and traditions abound

**Dysfunctional Family**

- ☑ Compulsively protecting feelings
- ☑ Existence of many taboo subjects
- ☑ Excessive control, criticism
- ☑ Use of shame as a punishment
- ☑ Voicing lots of should and shouldn'ts
- ☑ Unclear and inconsistent rules
- ☑ Rigidity and inflexibility
- ☑ A tense atmosphere
- ☑ Lots of anger
- ☑ Discouraging growth
- ☑ Discouraging healthy risk taking
- ☑ Perpetuating low self esteem

## Unwritten & Unspoken Rules

*"Rules are not necessarily sacred, principles are."*
**Franklin Roosevelt**

All systems, including families, classrooms and treatment programs live by a code of unwritten or unspoken rules. These rules are often replicated and are seldom given much thought. These "rules" exist for all, and children learn these rules through modeling and implicit messages; rarely are they verbalized.

**Don't talk about problems**. Children learn to avoid stating the obvious. This rule has been referred to as the "elephant in the living room" syndrome. You live around it, see it, smell it, but no one says that there is an elephant in the living room. Families living with this rule rarely discuss problems, preferring to let them blow over. Many subjects become taboo. Yet, they are there the next morning.

**Indirect communication is best**. Family members are taught to be indirect in their statements and avoid the intimacy that comes with direct communication. In some families, the children are taught to kick under the table or mutter under their breath. Passive-aggressive behavior may also exist, with members getting even with the others clandestinely. Another method of indirect communication is the telegraph process by which one person tells a second person what needs to be said to a third person.

**Not all feelings are acceptable**. A dysfunctional family teaches children to ignore certain feelings. A great deal of discounting is done, and children may be told that they should not feel a certain way. Children learn to edit their feelings, eventually losing touch with their emotions or becoming emotionally shutdown. "If you can't say something nice, say nothing at all."

**Appearances outweigh feelings**. This rule implies that what people think of you is more important than how you feel. This occurs when families care more about what the neighbors think than how their children feel. Statements and questions such as, "You've ruined the family name", and "What will our neighbors think?" are indicative.

**Do as I say, not as I do**. Primarily through modeling, children are taught to behave and act a certain way, while being told something different. Perhaps a parent will lecture a child on honesty, only to turn around and demonstrate dishonesty, or preach against drugs, while misusing alcohol.

**Don't be playful**. Remember, actions speak louder than words. In many families, survival is such that some children lose their spontaneity and ability to have fun (unless aided by chemicals), creating a "little adult" who is always serious. This is unfortunate because play is important to the emotional, physical, and social development of a child, adolescent and adult.

**Don't rock the boat**. In dysfunctional families, children learn to avoid saying or doing anything that may upset the family. This means the family members deny their own needs and desires, bite their tongues, and ignore their feelings. Though this rule is prevalent, one member is expected to rock the boat as part of his or her survival role (see scapegoat).

## We learn what we:

*See*
*Hear*
*Do*

## Survival Roles in School

When looking at a family system that is experiencing dysfunction, you must remember that there is a problem. In these families, the tendency is for the members to avoid looking at the real problem by focusing elsewhere. By having *survival roles* in place, the family is able to avoid the task of resolving that which is causing pain. This approach may deter healthy emotional growth and development, but it often feels safer than dealing with the true problem. As an educator, counselor or parent, you have seen these roles at school. When struggling with dysfunction, the family members go throughout their day remaining somewhat locked into their perspective roles. This may be seen in school, church, social or civic clubs and work.

The term *survival roles* refer to the set of compulsive behaviors that family members adopt to protect themselves from the emotional distress generated within the family system. *Survival roles* vary considerably and are seldom consciously adopted. Generally, the development of these roles is a reaction to a complex set of dynamics in the family.

## The *survival roles* serve two primary needs

> 1. They protect the individual from distress.
> 2. They help the family stay balanced, the status quo is maintained.

All families have these roles to some extent, and almost everyone can recognize the roles in their own family. The key to remember is that when a family is dysfunctional, the roles become compulsive. Individuals are stuck with a certain role, whether they like it or not. In healthy families, children trade roles easily and no one is locked into any one way of acting. An analogy for these roles might be that they are overcoats worn to protect—ideally, the overcoat can be removed when no longer essential. With dysfunctional families, children are unable to remove their overcoats, regardless of the consequences or their desire to change. Birth order and gender also have a predictable influence on the roles, regardless of the degree of health or dysfunction.

> Labels are for the convenience of the labeler. They are not helpful to students and tend to give an expectation to live up (or down) to.

When we try to make people fit according to labels, it rarely works. The following *survival roles* are descriptive and not an attempt to be diagnostic. It does not help children to create new labels for them to live up (or down) to. As you read about the different roles, understand that each one is named in order to keep some perspective and acknowledge that there are predictable components of each role. For the reader's benefit, we have assigned names to these roles, not as an attempt to create categories in which students must fit, but so we can contrast these roles and gain a better understanding of why students from the same family can be so different. The names of the *survival roles* that we will examine are: *Drill Sergeant, Caretaker, Scapegoat, Lost Child, Vulnerable Child, and Class Clown.*

Each role meets a different need for the family. The roles are distinct, but on the feeling level we see similarities. The more pronounced the feelings, the more compulsive the role becomes. Remember, the unwritten rules often prevent discussion or even acknowledgement that the feelings exist.

Though these survival roles are often seen in families struggling with severe issues such as chemical dependency, chronic depression and compulsive gambling, it has been observed that the same dynamics exist in families that are considered career military or fundamentally religious. What appears to be the common denominator is that an outside factor holds a great deal of sway over how the family functions. It seems when a family is bound by rigid or unrelenting expectations, the survival roles emerge in a way that is consistent with families suffering from problems that result in rigidity and oppression.

With that said, we all know families that have a long term association with the military or fundamental religion that are not dysfunctional. It would be an error to interpret the above observation as a slap toward the military or religion. Provided members are allowed flexibility, unconditional love, clear communication and consistent expectations, families can weather a great deal of distress and remain functionally healthy. Unfortunately, by these standards, a large percentage of families can be considered dysfunctional, whether there is a severe problem or not.

# The Smith Family

You are about to meet five children up close and personal. Consider it one of those brief encounters that come and go in our lives. Although information regarding family survival roles is provided; they need to come alive on these pages, even if temporarily. In the Smith family, dad is alcoholic and mom is struggling with the emotional wreckage to their family caused by his disease. The following is not about the parents; it is about the children, and the roles often adopted. The children range in age nine to nineteen, with all living at home but the oldest. Here are their words.

# Martha the Hero

My name is Martha; I am a girl. Well, I mean you can tell from my name, but I was told to include my gender when asked to write this. It's not that I think people are dumb. Then again, you haven't met my younger brother Felix. He's not really stupid, but something is wrong with him. All he does is get in trouble at school. I was so embarrassed last year when we were in the same high school. Anyway, this is supposed to be about me, so I better move on to more serious things.

I'm the oldest of five, but I no longer live at home. I am in college; I received a scholarship to Purdue University and am studying to be a social worker. I love school, but leaving home was probably the hardest thing I have ever done. I sometimes lie awake at night worried that something bad will happen at home and I won't be there to deal with it. Last year, I was asked out by some really cute guys, but never went because I was needed at home. No one told me to, but it just didn't feel right being gone. I thought it was selfish to go on a date when total chaos might break out at any time at home. I call home at least three times a week, sometimes every day. Mom says everything is okay; but, I don't always believe her. She is not a liar; she tries to hide problems from us. What is weird about that is she knows that I know. I used to stay up late with her when dad did not come home. Mom would swing between saying really mean things about dad and crying on my shoulder. When he is home, they fight all the time. I don't know why she worries about him, he doesn't worry about us. I guess she's confused. She doesn't deserve any of what she goes through.

As long as I was home, I felt that my brothers and sisters were okay. Not now; I'm worried that something will go wrong and I won't be able to fix it. Last year, I was honored at school for being in the top ten percent academically. I was senior class vice-president and played volleyball. I got a card from mom that said, "Don't think we don't know what you have done." It was one of the few times I can remember hearing something like that. I have to admit, I did cry some. However, as the time passed, I found myself feeling angry. I just don't know who I am angry with, my father and his drinking, my mother and her lack of care, or me for not being able to do anything about it. Maybe I should have tried harder.

# Drill Sergeant

## The child who assumes this role
- Is often the oldest child.
- Has a strong sense of responsibility for the everyday maintenance of the family.
- Is often seen as pushy and somewhat dominant.
- Ensures that everything is taken care of.
- Does not generate negative attention.
- Takes care of those things that the parent(s) no longer can or will, such as making sure dinner is prepared, homework completed, hands washed, rooms clean, etc.
- Often develops perfectionist behaviors and exaggerated sense of responsibility.
- Feels guilty, ashamed, remorseful, angry, and inadequate; no matter what the accomplishment, there is the sense that it could have been done better.

## The Drill Sergeant role meets the system's needs by
- Making things run smoothly.
- Perpetuating the illusion that things are normal and OK in the family.
- Minimizing the consequences of the real problem.

## The Drill Sergeant role meets the child's needs by
- Providing a sense of contribution and importance.
- Protecting against emotional pain through compulsive behaviors.

## In school the Drill Sergeant
- Is responsible.
- Is compelled to take control.
- Dominates by talking.
- Is parental and/or bossy with other students.
- Is disappointed with losing (or coming in second).
- Feels superior when winning.

## When working with a child who has assumed the role of the Drill Sergeant, do
- Give attention at times when the student is not achieving.
- Validate the person.

- Separate the person from his or her behavior.
- Let the student know it's OK to make mistakes.

**Don't**
- Let the student monopolize the conversation or let the student always be first.
- Validate his or her worth based on achievements.

## Caretaker

**The child who assumes this role**
- Has feelings that are very similar to the Drill Sergeant's, but the behavior is quite different.
- Takes responsibility for the day-to-day well-being of the family, primarily as the "fixer of dilemmas".
- Feels responsible for the hurt in the family, even though he or she did not cause it.
- Takes whatever steps are needed to make things OK.
- Is very nurturing and supportive of others, which often prevents him or her from meeting his or her own needs.
- Has profound empathy for brothers, sisters, and at times, strangers, and minimal concern for self.
- Takes responsibility for the emotional state of the family; since the child did not create the dysfunction, he or she has overwhelming feelings of failure and inadequacy.
- Has feelings of guilt, shame, remorse, anger, and inadequacy, and when asked what he or she needs, the answer is usually, "nothing, but I'm worried about my little brother or sister".
- Is viewed positively by others.

**The Caretaker role meets the system's needs by**
- Providing a peace-keeper and nurturer.
- Reducing distress and minimizing the emotional consequences of the real problem.

**The Caretaker role meets the child's needs by**
- Allowing for a sense of giving and selflessness.
- Contributing to a sense of taking care of others.

**In school the Caretaker**
- Tends to always volunteer.
- Has strong need for teacher attention and approval.
- Needs to be helpful.
- Worries about how others treat the teacher.

**When working with a child who has assumed the role of the Caretaker, do**

- Give attention at times when the student is not achieving.
- Validate the person and separate the person from the behavior.
- Let the student know it is okay to make mistakes.

**Don't**

- Let the student monopolize the conversation.
- Let the student always be first when volunteering.
- Validate worth based on achievements.

## Felix the Scapegoat

You are lucky I am even writing this crud. When first asked, I not only said no, but I cussed and walked away from the dude. What's the point of telling people who I am, when no one really gives a crap anyway? But, what the hell, here I go.

My name is Felix. I hate my name and friends call me "stealer". That has nothing to do with the football team from Pittsburg. You can figure it out on your own; at least those of you with half a brain. I just turned eighteen and a junior in high school. I failed third grade, which was a bunch of crap. That teacher didn't like me. Big deal, I didn't like him either; he was a jerk.

Like I said, I'm a junior and school sucks. Right now, strange things are happening in my house. First of all, my sister left; just went away. I don't blame her one bit. We fought and all that stuff, but she was okay and I kind of miss her. One big thing I miss is her doing stuff around here. Sometimes it would make me mad (I was asked not to cuss, but I want to) because she acted like she was my mother . . . she's only two years older. There were a lot of days that she got the little ones to school. She even cooked dinner at times. I don't know if she liked doing it, but it was always because mom was sleeping from the pills the doctor gave her for her nerves. There is no way I'm cooking dinner; so far mom's done it, or we've gotten a bucket of fried chicken from down the road. I like that, but I kind of wish we were all sitting down eating together. I've never said this to anyone, but I miss my dad; well, sort of. I also can't stand the way he is when drunk.

I was told to be open when writing this, that my last name isn't allowed. Big deal, how many Felix's are there with one brother and three sisters? I don't like being told how to do things. Plus, I don't care what people know about me, or my family. I could give a crap. Anyway, I got busted this summer with weed. It wasn't much, just a couple of joints I had already rolled. Some of us were down at the park doing nothing, and a couple of cops show up. One dude split and ran from the cops and that was stupid. He still got caught. It was kind of dark and I tried to get rid of it, but one of them saw me toss the joints behind me, in the tall grass. I went to jail because of a couple of stupid joints. That was bullcrap. What a stupid law. There were guys in there that had beat up the girlfriends, robbed stores, drove drunk. I never did any of those things.

Mom bailed me out the next morning, and I got on probation for six months. I'm still on it. I also had to pay a fine and mom took care of that. Sometimes she's cool like that. I wish my dad was like her. At least in how she comes to the rescue.

# Scapegoat

## The child that assumes this role
- Demonstrates defiance, rebellion, and anti-authority posture.
- Breaks the rules and rocks the boat within the system.
- Is often automatically blamed, even when innocent.
- Attracts negative attention so that the system avoids looking at the real problem.
- Acts out so that the family has a focus and someone to blame.
- Is unaware (as are all the others) of the role.
- Believes that the reason that he or she gets in trouble so much is because he or she is bad.
- Naturally carries the role into the classroom.
- Is rarely redirected by traditional consequences.
- Feels guilty, ashamed, angry, inadequate, and mistreated.
- Often pays a high price and experiences academic, social, and legal consequences.

## The Scapegoat role meets the system's needs by
- Creating a focus that allows the family to ignore the real problem.
- Providing someone to take the blame.

## The Scapegoat role meets the child's needs by
- Creating a sense of power and identity.
- Allowing the child to be more honest (sometimes brutally so).
- Allowing for strong peer relationships.

## In school the Scapegoat
- Blames others.
- Makes strong peer alliances.
- Act outs irritating behaviors.
- Is often rigid, defiant, and irresponsible.
- Has repeated discipline violations.
- Talks back to authority.
- Gets very little work done.
- Causes the staff to spend an inordinate amount of time focused on behaviors.

**When working with a child who has assumed the role of Scapegoat, do**

- Let the student know when behavior is inappropriate.
- Validate when the student takes responsibility for anything.
- See that the student is emotionally hurting—empathize.
- Set limits and give clear explanations of the student's responsibilities.
- Help the student understand that the behavior is his or her responsibility.
- Consistently follow through with consequences.

**Don't**

- Get hooked by the student's anger.
- Feel sorry for the student.
- Treat the student as special or with kid gloves.
- Personalize the inappropriate behavior.

## Melissa the Lost Child

There's really not much to say. My life is kind of boring and I read a whole lot. I love to read. I read about all kinds of stuff. Mostly, I like fiction where the guy and girl fall in love and everything is good. Reading isn't the only thing I do. I also like to draw. I got everything a person needs to draw. I got a drawing board in the corner, where it fits just right. I like drawing horses. Enough, I'm supposed to tell you about me.

I'm fifteen. a girl. I do well in school because I like to study in my room. My English teacher tells me I am smart and wants me to answer questions aloud. I know the answers; I just don't like to raise my hand. There are plenty of big mouths in class that like to do that anyway. I actually know the answers when no one else does, but am too nervous to say it.

I have a best friend, and her name is Shawna. We've been friends since second grade when they moved here from St. Paul. Her dad does something with software and his company moved them here. How lucky am I? Other than Shawna, there are people I sometimes say hello at school. They are in the drama class in fourth period with me. I love this class. I can act pretty good, and always remember my lines. My favorite part is this loudmouth lady. I might join the drama department this next semester. I need to figure out a ride home, but it would really be cool to be in real plays that have curtain calls, and stuff like that.

Let's see. I told you my name, how old I am. You know I am girl and like to draw and read. The only other thing I can tell you is that I am the middle kid. There are two above me and two below. I can't think of anything more to include. I keep my room perfect. The rest of the house is kind of messy. Instead of being around the mess, I just go to my room and draw. I'm not that good, but I can come to my room all the time practice, practice, practice. That is how people get better, by doing things a bunch of times. I have all the time in the world to do that.

# Lost Child

## The child who assumes this role
- Often avoids conflict.
- Is reserved, shy, and introspective.
- Attempts to meet his or her own emotional needs through prolific reading or active fantasy, etc.
- Is often observed as creative.
- Has a tendency to prefer solitude.
- May be easily overlooked and often forgotten.
- May seem to strive for anonymity, yet also desire more attention.
- Will rarely demand attention, negative or positive.
- Will rarely raise his or her hand in class even though he or she knows the answer.
- May be overweight because of the need for nurturing. If nurturing isn't gained through affection, it may come from eating.
- Feels lonely, unloved, insignificant, sad, and inadequate.

## The Lost Child role meets the family's needs by
- Generating very little turmoil.
- By not creating problems so the family can continue to blame the scapegoat and avoid looking at the dysfunction.
- Giving the family the sense that everything is OK.

## The Lost Child role meets the child's needs by
- Offering a sanctuary of privacy and introspection.
- Allowing the child to emotionally disengage from the family, so that the child feels less distress.
- Keeping feelings internalized and rarely acknowledged.

## In school the Lost Child
- Will stay quiet and reserved, the so-called wallflower.
- Is rarely a behavior problem.
- Will have few friends.
- Is often creative and enjoys art, music, poetry, and writing.
- Often appears to have poor or untested social skills.
- May be ignored or teased by other students.

**When dealing with a child who has assumed the role of Lost Child, do**

- Make a special effort to refer to him or her by name.
- Attempt one-on-one contact.
- Establish a relationship.
- Point out and encourage the student's strengths and talents.
- Be aware of his or her creativity.
- Pick up on his or her interests—it gives him or her permission to talk.
- Use touch cautiously, in safe places (shoulder, arm, etc.).
- Help the student build relationships.
- Encourage working in small groups to build trust and confidence.

**Don't**

- Let the student off the hook because of silence—wait for an answer.
- Let others take care of the student by answering for him or her.

## Preston the Class Clown

My name is Presto and I'm a magician. Just kidding. My real name is Preston. I think Presto would be kind of cool for a name. I can hear it now, "Presto, could you stand up", and every kid in class stand-ups like she said a magic word. It would be, "Presto" this, "Presto that". The best would be if for some reason the teacher would say, "Presto you can go to the restroom now." I doubt I could get everybody to pee at one time, but it would be the coolest thing ever. I know Jerry and David would do it. They can do crazy things as well.

I'm eleven, have one brother and three sisters, and am in fifth grade. Next year I go to middle school and will have five or six classes, instead of just one main teacher like now. I have a bunch of practical jokes I can do on all my new teachers. Ms. Mills sometimes laughs at things I say, even though I can tell she is trying hard not to. My favorite things to do are hang out with buddies and play video games. I can flip my eyelids inside out, move my ears without touching them and burp on purpose. I've tried to do my ABCs, but only got as far as L before my burp runs out. I bet there aren't many people who can do all of that. I do okay with my grades. I could do better, but I really don't spend much time studying or doing my homework good. Everyone says I could do better and be more like my oldest sister. No way! She's boring, hardly ever smiles and is always doing stuff that adults do. Like cleans and cooks, gives rides . . . all kinds of things mom used to do. She's at college now and things aren't working out around here as much. The second kid, Felix is hanging around more and helping out. Probably because he's on probation and wears an ankle thing so a satellite can track his every movement. There's probably an F.B.I. guy making sure he stops being such a loser.

Right below me is Loretta. If I were to describe her, I'd say a wimp, cries all the time, is pouty and doesn't do nothing around here. It's always someone else getting her dirty clothes off the floor in her room and even answering for her when she takes too long to answer herself. It's kind of mean to say all those things. She's not that bad, but when I need help with homework, she's always getting it instead. If I had a dollar for every time I heard, "I'll be there when finished with Loretta", I'd be rich. For real, if I got money for every time that was said, I'd be asking for help with everything I do. Help me chew, help me scratch, help me walk, help me help you. Notice I did not include going to the restroom. You couldn't pay me a million dollars to ask someone to help me there. Now, two million, that's a different story.

# Class Clown

**The child who assumes this role**

- Has a tendency to joke and use humor to the point of being inappropriate.
- May be unable to be serious, even when the situation demands it.
- Is well liked by peers.
- Is rarely expected to be responsible.
- Is avoided when dependability and empathy are desired.
- Uses humor to minimize and deny fear.

**The Class Clown role meets the family's needs by**

- Providing relief from distress.
- Entertaining the family.

**The Class Clown role meets the child's needs by**

- Warding off painful feelings through humor.
- Generating social acceptance.

**In school the Class Clown**

- Is funny and distracting.
- Gets attention with funny faces, comments, and practical jokes.
- Likes to entertain others and may come across as immature.
- Has a hard time coping when a situation gets serious.

**When dealing with a child who has assumed the role of Class Clown, do**

- Be honest with your feelings.
- Encourage an appropriate sense of humor.
- Expect responsible behavior.
- Encourage him or her to talk about feelings.
- Hold accountable.

**Don't**

- Laugh at inappropriate behavior—it invalidates you.
- Personalize the comments he or she makes in class.
- Lower your expectations regarding participation.
- Try to deny how funny this person can be.

## Loretta the Vulnerable Child

Just so people know, Loretta is telling me what to write and I'm doing that for her. She came into my room when I was drawing, and asked me if I could help her write this. I don't mind. She's only nine and it would take a thousand years for her to do it. Here is what Loretta said:

My name is Loretta May and I am nine years old. I am in the second grade at Sherman elementary school. I have two older brothers and two sisters. I like cats and have twelve cat books on my shelf. Our cat is named Sissy and I named her myself. Sissy is really a boy, but he doesn't really know he has a girl's name. My favorite subject is art and my worst class is math. My favorite vacation place is the Magic Kingdom at Disney World. We haven't been there yet, but two years ago, dad said we were going. I bet this summer we go. Everybody loves Mickey Mouse and Goofy. The rest are okay, but my favorites are Mickey Mouse and Goofy the dog. We do go to my aunt Bella's house most every summer, but we haven't been there for two years in a row.

School is okay and I like it most of the time. One thing I don't like is that my teacher never asks me to do things like run a note to the office, or take a paper to Ms. Kutack in the next room over. She has even looked right at me and still picked someone else. It's just like at home, even before I am finished my chores, someone takes over. It is almost like I am not there. I get good grades on homework because people help me, but haven't learned the stuff. That is when I don't want Mrs. Hightower to select me to do a problem at the board. At the first of the year, she asked me two times if I wanted to do the problem for the class. Both times, I shook my head and stopped looking at her.

My family used to sit down at the table and have dinner together most nights. I really like that. One of the older kids would say the blessing and people most of the time would talk, cut up and laugh. Other times when I looked around the table, I would see Martha cutting my food, Felix looking mad about something, Melissa was just eating and Preston was messing around with his food and showing people. He asked me if I liked seafood. I said yes and he opened his mouth that was yucky and said, "see". It was gross and everyone else still laughed, even Martha kind of smiled.

We don't eat together anymore. Daddy doesn't come home until late and my mom tries to sleep. Martha is gone, Felix is a jerk, Melissa likes to read and paint, Preston can't be serious and I still get words spelled around me like I can't spell. I know what is going on around here. I may be young, but I am not stupid and blind.

# Vulnerable Child

## The child that assumes this role
- Is referred to as the baby of the family.
- Is often the youngest family member.
- Appears convinced that he or she is fragile and unable to be responsible.
- Is rarely allowed to make decisions independently.
- Is rarely given responsibility for self or others.
- Is viewed as vulnerable and incapable by the entire family system.

## The Vulnerable Child role meets the family's needs by
- Providing a seemingly fragile, helpless individual that demands primary concern and attention taking the focus off the true problem.
- As long as everyone in the family continues to treat this person as fragile, he or she can avoid looking at his/her fears or concerns. If you or I were on a sinking ship and someone handed us an infant, our focus would shift to the child. Our lives would still be in peril, but our primary concern would be for the little one. This is the role the Vulnerable Child provides for the family system.

## The Vulnerable Child role meets the child's needs by
- Convincing everyone, including teachers, that he or she cannot be relied on to be responsible.
- Placing few demands on an already overwhelmed child.

## In school the Vulnerable Child
- Is unwilling to take risks.
- Is easily emotionally hurt by others.
- Quits activities when he or she experiences difficulties.
- Seems overwhelmed and fragile.

## When dealing with a child who has assumed the role of the Vulnerable Child, do
- Establish eye contact.
- Develop a relationship.
- Encourage risk-taking in small groups.
- Hold the student accountable for participation.
- Maintain expectations.

**Don't**
- Let this student convince you that he or she is unable to complete a task.
- Accept the fragility—it is a distress pattern that can be interrupted.
- Treat this student as if he or she will break emotionally.

These roles are active in the classroom and explain the wide array of behaviors, from the student who is the super-volunteer to the one who tries to hide in the back. The role drives the behavior. As adults, we should see the child as separate from the role. The role is a result of birth order, not something written into a person's DNA.

The survival roles can also be seen at school with faculty members, or any other system that people operate within. Ordinarily the person is unaware of his or her role and assumes that "this is just the way I am". These roles do not fade away because we become adults.

## Make a Connection

Connect the statements with the family system role that best fits.

| | |
|---|---|
| **Drill Sergeant** | A. *"I'm the shy one in our family. I'd rather read than visit."* |
| **Care taker** | B. *"I could care less about who is happy or sad; I'm out of here."* |
| **Scapegoat** | C. *"I'm the responsible one; someone has to take care of things."* |
| **Lost child** | D. *"I can't do it; it's just too hard for me."* |
| **Class clown** | E. *"I'm sad when my little brother and sisters are sad."* |
| **Vulnerable child** | F. *"Hey, did you hear the one about the preacher an . . . "d prostitute?"* |
| | (Answers on the next page) |

The intent of this section on family systems is to underscore the power and influence of something the school has no control over. How parents choose

NOEL R. LOVE

to raise their children is not the school's business. How parents demonstrate love, discipline and affection is outside of the school's parameters. Yet, the family system has a huge impact on how students value learning, perceive education and treat others. Understanding some of the dynamics of family systems helps to make sense of why some kids do what they do at school. It also helps us to understand why some parents seem to resist the school's efforts.

Insight into any situation increases the ability to have a positive influence on certain dynamics. Knowing why some students behave in a particular manner and how that behavior meets needs that are often beyond the school is essential. Seeing and understanding family dynamics helps to answer questions that often are left unanswered: Why isn't she like her big sister? Why are the parents so resistant to supporting education? What can be done to get the parents on board with the school? Why does mom or dad blame the teacher when their child is struggling? Why won't mom call back when a teacher leaves a message?

Educators should know how their own family system impacts attitudes, values and actions. Why are some teachers rigid and unyielding? How come others are "pushovers" and let kids run all over them? What is the reason one teacher has a huge heart for children and another seems to have no heart? Knowing our survival roles helps us understand why we are the way we are now. It seems unlikely that one can possess too much insight into why he or she is a certain way. The lack of insight leaves us open to stumbling in relationships with others. An abundance of insight clears the way for much better navigation, even when the path is overgrown with the weeds of uncertainty and confusion.

Care taker (E), Drill sergeant (C), Scapegoat (B), Lost child (A), Class clown (F), Vulnerable child (D)

*"I am now the most miserable man living. If what I feel were equally distributed to the whole human family, there would not be one cheerful face on the earth. Whether I shall ever be better I can not tell; I awfully forebode I shall not. To remain as I am is impossible; I must die or be better, it appears to me".*
*Abraham Lincoln*

# Chapter 7

# Depression

Depression is common and affects most people at some point. Situational depression occurs when circumstances are such that discouragement, disappointment, sadness and hopelessness persist. Fortunately, this type of depression often clears when the situation or circumstance improves. Major Depression is defined as an illness when the feelings of sadness, hopelessness, and despair persist and interfere with a child, adolescent or adult's ability to function, regardless of the situation. Some form of depression is common in teens and younger children. Adolescence tends to generate certain angst and adolescents experience subsequent mood swings that at times can be fairly profound. One day we see giddiness and jubilation, and the next day we observe a quiet, flat affect that suggests a major shift in mood. It is important to not look at normal adolescent mood swings as pathological. There are many ups and downs during these years of growth, development, independence, maturation and self-discovery.

Situational *Depression* relates to what is going on around the student and tends to clear up when the situation improves. This type of depression can also exist when a student turns the anger he or she feels inward, rather than confronting the person or situation causing the feelings. Stuffing anger can result in a sense of depression. Most everyone has experienced this type of depression, and though it is painful to go through, it tends to pass eventually.

*Major Depressive Disorder* is a profound sense of discouragement, apathy or sadness that exists in spite of the environment. Chemical imbalance is believed to be at the root of much clinical depression and talk therapy alone is only partially successful. Neurotransmitters such as serotonin and dopamine exist at levels inconsistent with individuals who are not depressed. Or the levels are normal, but the ability for the brain to secrete and retrieve these chemicals is impeded. Modern medicine offers a physician or psychiatrist significant treatment options to accompany talk therapy.

## The Symptoms of Depression
### According to the National Institutes of Health

- Thoughts or expressions of suicide or self-destructive behavior
- Poor concentration
- Self-Injury
- Hopelessness
- Frequent sadness, tearfulness, crying
- Change in sleep or eating patterns
- Frequent complaints of physical illnesses, such as headaches and stomachaches
- Increased irritability, anger, or hostility
- Apathy
- Frequent absences from school or poor performance in school
- Persistent boredom, low energy
- Difficulty with relationships
- Low self esteem and guilt
- Isolation from peers
- Extreme sensitivity to rejection or failure
- Self medication with alcohol and other drugs
- Bleak outlook

## Statistics on Adolescent Depression
National Institute of Mental Health

- One in five children has some sort of mental, behavioral, or emotional problem.
- One in ten may have a serious emotional problem.
- One in eight may suffer from depression.
- Thirty percent who could benefit from help receive any sort of intervention or treatment.
- Seventy percent simply struggle through the pain of mental illness or emotional turmoil, doing their best to make it to adulthood.

Brown University reported in 2002 that many parents simply do not recognize the symptoms of depression in their adolescent children. They found that even parents who have good communication with their children do not necessarily realize when a child is depressed (The Brown University Child and Adolescent Behavior Letter, Vol. 18, No 4, April 2002).

*"Life and death are balanced on the edge of a razor."*
*Homer, Iliad*

## Untreated Depression can lead to . . .

Reckless behavior
Problems at school
Chemical use
Running away
Low self-esteem
Eating disorders
Self-injury
Internet dependency
Violence
Suicide

According to the American Academy of Child and Adolescent Psychiatry

After a decade of steady decline, in 2009, teenage suicide hit a fifteen-year high. It is the third leading cause of death for 15-to-24-year-olds, and the sixth leading cause of death for 5-to-14-year-olds.

## Some Indicators

- **Talking About Dying**—any mention of dying, disappearing, jumping, shooting oneself, or other types of self harm
- **Change in Personality**—sad, withdrawn, irritable, anxious, tired, indecisive, apathetic
- **Change in Behavior**—can't concentrate on school, work, routine tasks
- **Change in Sleep Patterns**—insomnia, often with early waking or oversleeping, nightmares
- **Change in Eating Habits**—loss of appetite and weight, or overeating

## Suicide Risk Factors

- **History of Mental Health Issues**—including depression and suicide in the family
- **Depressed**—ninety percent of kids who attempt suicide are either depressed or chemically dependent
- **Alcohol or other Drugs; Heavy Involvement**—with alcohol or other drugs
- **Previous Suicide Attempts**—about one-third of teen suicide victims have attempted it before
- **Ongoing Stressful Situations**—that the teen perceives as serious and "unfixable"
- **Knowing Other Teenagers**—who have died because of suicide. Kids who have recently read, seen or heard about suicide are more prone to try it.
- **Recent Loss**—through death, divorce, separation, broken relationship, self-confidence, self-esteem, loss of interest in friends, hobbies, activities previously enjoyed
- **Fear of losing control**—acting erratically, harming self or others
- **Low self esteem**—feeling worthless, shame, overwhelming guilt, self-hatred, "everyone would be better off without me"

- **No hope for the future**—believing things will never get better; that nothing will ever change

Other risk factors include a history of physical and/or sexual abuse, poor communication with parents, incarceration, and lack of access or an unwillingness to seek mental health treatment.

*"Talking about recovering from grief is almost disrespectful, as life never returns to the way it was before the loss of someone close. When people talk of recovery, they really refer to overcoming grief and adapting to life after death. This is an important distinction to draw, because the purpose of grief work is not to "get over" loss, but to adjust to its consequences, and restore balance."*

*P. Rich*

# Chapter 8

# Loss and Grief

Shattered dreams, death of a loved one and a broken heart can lead to a strong sense of loss. Moving to another community, experiencing a parents' divorce, terminating involvement with a strong interest, hobby or activity, can all lead to a sense of loss. Death more than anything results in a profound sense of grief for students, even when the student is only loosely associated with the deceased. When a parent, sibling, friend or relative dies, teens feel the overwhelming loss of someone who helped shape their self-identities. On some level these feelings about the death become a part of their lives forever.

Sad to say, many adults who lack understanding of their experiences discourage teens from sharing their grief. Bereaved teens exhibit all kinds of signs revealing they are struggling with complex feelings, yet are often pressured to act as if they are doing better than they really are. When a parent dies, many teens are told to "be strong" and "carry on" for the surviving parent. They may not know if they will survive themselves, let alone be able to support someone else. Obviously, these kinds of conflicts hinder the "work of mourning".

Teens are no longer children, yet neither are they adults. With the exception of infancy, no developmental period is so filled with change as adolescence. Leaving the security of childhood, the adolescent begins the process of separating from parents. The death of a parent or sibling can be a particularly devastating experience during this already difficult period. At the same time, the bereaved teen is confronted by the death of someone loved; he or she also faces psychological, physiological and academic pressures. While teens may begin to look like "men" or "women", they will still need consistent and compassionate support as they mourn; physical development does not always equal emotional maturity. Youth are usually expected to be "grown up" and support other members of the family, particularly a surviving parent and/or younger brothers and sisters. Many teens have been told, "Now you will have to take care of your family." When an adolescent feels responsible for the "care for the family", he or she does not have the opportunity or the permission to mourn for his or her own loss.

There are many reasons why healthy grieving can be especially difficult for teenagers. Some grieving teens may even behave in ways that seem inappropriate or frightening.

Below are three examples of kids who are grieving a loss. In each case, it wasn't the death of a family member that caused the hurt. Loving deeply isn't always restricted to immediate family. The loss of a passion, a pet or a best friend can have as big an impact as the loss of a person. Mark, Cynthia and Jean can attest to this.

## Losses of a Different Kind

## More Than a Game

Mark made a decision today that left him empty and sad. His mom needed help and as the oldest of four, he had to go to work after school. He had no choice; they were about to be evicted from their apartment. Going to work wasn't the hard part of his decision. The hard part was he had to tell Coach Jackson he was quitting the team. Out of all the things he did, being on the team was the most important to Mark. He loved being part of the team. He loved the connection and camaraderie he had with others. He was good at playing ball; it was the highlight of his life. Sadly, home life was not. His mom cried when it became clear Mark would have to quit the team; it devastated her that he had to. She knew what it meant to him. Ever since he began, Mark's eyes would light up when he talked about playing. Being part of the team, sharing something special with the other guys and feeling included made him proud. It would be all gone! Today a huge, empty hole was left inside Mark.

## Birds of a Feather

Cynthia didn't care that her family thought she was a bit overboard when it came to loving her cockatiel, Ronald. For some reason, out of the entire family, Ronald took to Cynthia and loved to sit on her shoulder when she watched TV, did her homework or completed her chores. Ronald would gently nudge his beak against her neck in an act of love. One day she got home and found out Ronald was a girl. Three little eggs were in a nest made of newspaper at the top of her bedroom closet. Cynthia knew the eggs would not hatch since there was no mate. Ronald did not know this and spent all day sitting on her eggs. Cynthia learned that both male and female Cockatiels shared the brooding and that Ronald wouldn't leave the nest until her mate took over. Ronald wouldn't eat if it meant abandoning the nest. Cynthia reached up, gently moved her bird out of the nest, and carefully covered the eggs with her own hand. Ronald flew off to her cage and ate; she trusted her. Ronald saw Cynthia as her mate. Cockatiels mate for life and Cynthia looked forward to the years she and Ronald would spend together. Last week, her cockatiel contracted a blood disease and died within forty-eight hours. Just like that, Cynthia lost a most precious part of her life. She wouldn't ever feel her bird land on her shoulder. Never again would Ronald nudge Cynthia's neck in that special way. Ronald was buried in the backyard with the whole family attending her funeral. Cynthia couldn't look at the top of her closet anymore; for a long time she kept expecting to see Ronald in her nest trying to hatch her eggs.

## Friends Forever and Ever

Jean had no idea she could feel this lonely. She was miserable and constantly thought about Marie moving away. Friends since first grade, Jean and Marie were like sisters, closer than most. They shared every secret together, talked about boys and how stupid brothers were. They had everything in common and were always together. Marie had always lived next door with her window facing Jean's. How many nights had they sat and talked after they were supposed to go to sleep. Jean never ever expected for Marie to move away. She figured they'd be best friends and even go to the same college and be roommates. A month ago, Marie's father was transferred to another state. The girls counted down the days until the moving van pulled up. Saying goodbye hurt in such a deep way that no one could console Jean. She lost her appetite, had trouble sleeping and couldn't concentrate at school. Jean lost the very best friend she thought she would ever have. Everything reminded her of Marie, particularly her window. No more late night talks. Jean had no idea she could feel so lonely.

Grief and loss will be presented in the classroom by students who don't know they are grieving. Grades, attendance and classroom behavior may all be impacted and it is important to watch for patterns that may suggest grief is apparent. How adults respond when a loved one dies has a major effect on the way young people react to the death. Sometimes adults don't want to talk about the death, assuming that by doing so, young people will be spared some of the pain and sadness. However, the reality is very simple: teens grieve anyway. Teens often need caring adults to confirm that it's all right to be sad and to feel a multitude of emotions when someone they love dies. They also usually need help understanding that the hurt they feel now won't last forever. When ignored, teens may suffer more from feeling isolated than from the actual death itself. Worse yet, they will probably feel all alone in their grief.

These statements tend to invalidate the feelings and thoughts the student is experiencing when grieving a loss.

## Those Dreaded Clichés You Really Do not Need to Say

*Your loved one is in a better place.*
*At least they don't have to suffer anymore.*
*If you look around, there's always someone worse off.*
*Keep your chin up!*
*You can handle it; you're strong and determined.*
*It was his or her time to go.*
*I know just how you feel.*
*Be thankful, you still have your mom . . .*
*You need to be strong for the family.*
*It's been six months; it's time for you to move on!*
*Count your blessings.*
*It is God's will!*

*"The place looked as though it had been visited by Genghis Kahn."*
**Terry Pratchett**

# Chapter 9

# Trauma

It is tiresome watching the news (24 hours a day), reading the newspaper or just hearing about the tragedies on the other side of the planet. There was a time when people were impacted only by the trauma in their tribes, villages or communities. Now instant information and the shrinking size of the world brings so many more tragedies to our table. We know trauma is not new; for centuries people have struggled with and dealt with its' impact on their lives. What is different today is the frequency of trauma, the increased risk factors and reduced or absent protective factors. Schools deal regularly with trauma and educators need effective tools and strategies to address the trauma. A variety of ways to respond to trauma need to be added to the tool belt of every educator. You never know when the right tool will come in handy. Trauma will be addressed from the point of view of the impact it has on grades, attendance and behavior.

The list below is not expected to add new or revealing information to the reader. Most know about the things that hurt children. It is here to emphasize the myriad of issues that are traumatic, supporting the concern that teachers *regularly* are charged with educating traumatized students.

- Chemical Dependency
- Divorce
- Racial Prejudice
- Sexual Abuse
- Loss and Grief
- Peer Conflicts
- Violence
- Target of Bullying
- Natural Catastrophes

- Physical Abuse
- Mental Illness
- Chronic Illness
- Eating Disorders
- Death
- Chronic Hunger
- Parental Rage or Neglect
- Severe Poverty
- Other (this list could go on)

*Taken in either large choking gulps or small caustic sips, trauma leaves a bitter taste.*

## Trauma Gets Most of Us Eventually

How many students in any American classroom experience some form of trauma? The question is somewhat rhetorical since trauma is so common it doesn't seem to warrant any attempt to prove its' existence with hard data. Those who work with youth know anecdotally that trauma affects a great number of kids. But, how many? First, we need to establish what is considered trauma.

## Drawing a Picture of Trauma

By definition, trauma is the sudden and often unexpected occurrence of an emotionally staggering or physically destructive event. Strong feelings are spawned, quite often without the person's awareness. When the trauma is chronic (occurs over an extended period), children can develop Post Traumatic Stress Disorder (PTSD), exacerbating the existing symptoms that already exist. There is a difference between trauma and PTSD, even if vague. A divorce provokes different levels of trauma than does repeated violence in the home, or the witnessing of a suicide attempt by a loved one (which doesn't necessarily result in PTSD).

Physical trauma is apparent and can include a loss of a limb, a major injury resulting from violence, maimed bodies, severe burns or war wounds. What about emotional trauma? Issues such as sexual abuse and physical abuse are clearly traumatic. Absolutely no question there! But is it traumatic to live through the parents' divorce? After all, fifty percent of marriages end in divorce in this country. Certainly, something as common as a family splitting up can't be that traumatic, or can it? Those who have survived one (or two, three . . .), might strongly argue that it is.

## You Can Run, But You Cannot Hide!

We know children need safe homes and communities, structure and boundaries, healthy role models and a healthy relationship with an adult other than the parents. They need to be valued by society, to attend caring schools, to engage in service activities and to be secure in their surroundings and neighborhoods. More than ever before, the lack of protective factors and developmental assets makes it more difficult to handle trauma. It is no exaggeration to say that by the age of eighteen, most people will experience some level of trauma. *The American Journal of Public Health* (Volume 90, Number 1) reports that more than one in four U.S. children (19 million children or 28.6 percent) are exposed to a home impacted by the disease of alcoholism: a home where hopes are often dashed, dreams shattered, promises broken, and trust destroyed. *The American Academy of Child & Adolescent Psychiatry* states that sexual abuse of children is reported more than 80,000 times annually. Experts believe this is the tip of the iceberg. It is speculated that up to one-third of children in the U.S. will at some time be touched inappropriately by an adult, very often someone well known. When we include some of the more toxic aspects of our culture such as violence, racism, gang war, bullying and road rage, we see that trauma is sadly a part of our daily lives, taken in either large choking doses, or small caustic sips. Either way, it leaves a bitter taste. These traumatized students then come to school to learn.

*"All children have to be deceived if they are to grow up without trauma."*
**Kazuo Ishiguro**

## Post Traumatic Stress Disorder

Post Traumatic Stress Disorder is a medically recognized occurrence to a highly stressful situation, either physical or emotional. The key is recognizing the child experiences tremendous fear or helplessness. Post Traumatic Stress Disorders can occur with people of all ages and has a damaging affect on school, relationships, interests and mental health. PTSD in children can occur because of natural disasters (tornadoes, hurricanes, and floods) or those that are man-made such as war, murder, rape, targeted school shootings, car or plane accidents, community-based violence, and physical injury such as severe burns, sexual or physical abuse and suicide. For each, there may be varying degrees on how it affects a person. We are all different and possess different degrees of resiliency.

## To Carry the Load or Not

As educators, being overwhelmed by the recurrence of student trauma is very understandable; this alone is one of the best arguments for self care. There is a tendency for some adults to carry the problem and pain on their own shoulders. Some self-protect, pull back or develop a "thick skin". This is not a problem when infrequent and short-lasting. What can disable an educator's ability to respond well to trauma is when long-term reactions persist. Caring about someone who has been traumatized demands emotional energy. Just hearing or being informed about a person, even a stranger who experiences trauma can result in being "mini-traumatized". Incidents on television news shows or in the newspaper are digested one at a time and are not too sour to chew. But these can accumulate, creating quite a bit more emotional indigestion than expected. We can burnout, walk away, drink too much, quit caring or be sad and discouraged most of the time. Or, another option is to engage in self care (See page 251).

## Signs and Symptoms of PTSD

The signs and symptoms listed below are a compilation of what may occur when students experience PTSD. The effects of trauma usually appear within a day to three months after the traumatic event. With some people it may take years before it manifests. This delay warns us about assuming that following the trauma the student should be better, no longer displaying symptoms. The belief that a student is "milking" the situation or malingering just adds insult to injury by rubbing salt into a wound. Often the behavior is similar to other trauma, but PTSD tends to last longer and be more difficult to recover from without help.

## *Potential signs of a person suffering from PTSD

- Decrease in activities and other valued enjoyments.
- Detachment from others.
- Sense of hopelessness about the present and future.
- Reoccurring dreams or flashbacks about the event.
- Distress at anniversaries of the trauma.
- Avoidance of people, places and things associated with the trauma.
- Emotional shut down with diminished ability to feel.
- Regression in development such as the need for toilet training or engaging in baby-talk.
- Physical and psychological hypersensitivity (not present before the trauma) with at least two of the following reactions:
  - o trouble sleeping
  - o anger
  - o difficulty concentrating
  - o exaggerated startle-response to noise
  - o physiological reaction to situations that approximate the traumatic event

**\*Mayo Foundation (2009)**

*"Coke and rum. Got weed on the ton."*
**50 Cent**

*"Whiskey river take my mind"*
**Willie Nelson**

# Chapter 10

# Drinking and Drugging

Several years ago, a state legislator tried to sponsor a bill requiring all certified secondary teachers to become licensed chemical dependency counselors. It failed! The only argument that can be made for such a hyper-vigilante effort is the high frequency teachers come into contact with students who are under the influence. He figured that since a teacher spent so much time around kids who used alcohol and other drugs, he or she needed to have a professional understanding of the problem. Well intended, but poorly considered. Based on that argument teachers also need to become nutritionists, family therapists, eye, ear and nose specialists, social workers, pastors, and everyone's mom or dad.

Plates are full, putty is stretched to the point of breaking, and heads are barely above water already with too much interference by those who don't teach. It seems people have forgotten that the purpose of school is to teach children. Our classroom teachers need support, not accusations and hindrances. This section is only to inform the reader of some basic facts about teenage drug and alcohol use. No one is asked to become a counselor, make a diagnosis, or solve the age old problem of chemicals in our society. Yet, anyone who works with kids should be aware of outcomes and consequences of alcohol and other drug use.

In 1956, The American Medical Association declared that alcoholism is a medical disease. This is not debated in this book. When an alcoholic is treated as if he has a disease, we see successful recovery. When treated as a symptom of some underlying psychiatric disorder, alcoholics rarely get sober. This statement applies to those who are diagnosed as chemically dependent. Abstinence is vital for someone with this disease to get better. Attempts at controlled use fail over and over again. Either it is complete abstinence, or out of control use. As it is said, "one drink is too many and one hundred not enough." When chemical dependency is treated as a lack of will power, the finger pointing, shaming and condemning do not help the recovery process. On the contrary, these kinds of strategies often result in social isolation, shunning and increased drinking or drugging.

Of the four categories covered, only one can be considered a disease, chemical dependency; most people who drink and drug fall within one of the other three categories: *experimentation, seeking the mood swing, and harmful involvement.*

In this section, we will also explore some of the contradictory messages our children are exposed to regarding alcohol and other drugs. There is no argument that people under twenty-one simply should not ingest any mood altering chemicals. Based on research, some suggest that instead of twenty-one, the minimum age of consent should be no less than twenty-five. Imagine the stink this would cause our liquor industry if we changed the minimum age of consent.

## The Center on Alcohol Marketing and Youth at Georgetown University has found that:

- In 2007, more than 40% of youth exposure to alcohol advertising on television came from ads placed on youth-oriented programming, that is, programs with disproportionately large audiences of 12-to-20-year-olds.
- In 2007, approximately one out of every five alcohol advertisements was placed on programming that youth ages 12 to 20 were more likely per capita to see than adults of the legal drinking age.[2] Almost all of these placements were on cable television, where distilled spirits companies in particular have dramatically increased their alcohol advertising in the past seven years.
- Evidence that exposure to alcohol advertising and marketing increases the likelihood of underage drinking has grown substantially. Since 2001, at least seven peer-reviewed longitudinal studies have found that young people with greater exposure to alcohol marketing are more likely to start drinking than their peers.
- Between 2001 and 2007, alcohol companies aired 73,565 "responsibility" advertisements on television. Youth ages 12 to 20 were 22 times more likely to see an alcohol product advertisement than an alcohol-industry-funded "responsibility" advertisement.

American children spend more time watching television than they spend in the classroom; they see an average of 2,000 beer commercials a year. Some samples of the messages presented in alcohol commercials are:

### Our product will make you . . .

Sexy
Loyal
Funny
Healthy
Popular
Intelligent
Successful
Adventurous

**Messages from major pharmaceutical companies via television commercials**

## You never have to feel bad

Cannot sleep, take this.
Cannot stay awake, take this.
Eat too much, take this.
Have a headache, take this.
Feel sad, take this.
Leg twitching, take this.
Trouble concentrating, take this.
Cannot have sex, take this.
Getting old, take this.

Quick fix and "band-aid" attitudes toward health abound. Major drug manufacturers sell billions of dollars worth of products per year. Still, we confuse our children with the statement that drugs are bad and that they should be eliminated. Well, which is it? Is the issue black and white, or are their considerable gray areas, where the questions demand more than simple slogans and political rhetoric? The prevention messages we send regarding chemical use are inconsistent with the attitudes and beliefs that our children are bombarded with on a daily basis.

There is no question that drug misuse is a serious problem, slowly consuming some of our precious children. However, there has never been a time when America was drug free. Alcohol, opium and hemp go back to the first boatload of European settlers. Tobacco was introduced by Native Americans and soon became the rave across the Atlantic. In fact, there has never been a time on our planet that mood altering chemicals did not exist and were not consumed. Eight thousand years ago, ancient texts described building a fire, throwing rocks on it and a building a tent over it. The ancient texts also described the people throwing handfuls of hemp on the rocks and sitting around getting high. Prior to the Inuit being exposed to alcohol, it was the only culture totally and completely drug free. This wasn't based on some moral decision; they couldn't obtain it up in the frozen north. Of course, this changed rather drastically once alcohol was made available through trade.

Without a doubt, the use of some substances has increased dramatically over time. During the time when several revolutions were going on, such as the sexual revolution and women's lib, there was another cultural revolution going on. "Tune in, turn on and drop out" was a posture suggested by a professor from the University of California, Timothy Leary.

As the use of mind-altering chemicals increased, society scrambled for a solution. It is interesting to note that attempts to make a particular substance difficult to get, quite often increased its power and status, creating a paradoxical effect. The use of drugs exploded! Prior to this, opium had been available in laudanum (used for numerous ills), hemp was available and even sold in mail order catalogs (put into candy to be eaten) and cocaine was detected in what we'd call household items. Who hasn't heard that *Coke* used to contain coke? Basically a very old activity that had been around for centuries became a contemporary nightmare. Courts are log jammed, jails are filled to capacity, hundreds of prisons have been built and millions have been spent on prevention. During this time, dads are taken from families, moms left to carry on, children are crying themselves to sleep, schools are suspending thousands and sons and daughters are lost to the dark night. Laws, slogans, fifteen second commercials on television, the creation of a national Drug Czar and the Drug Enforcement Agency have been impotent (it isn't a typo). The emperor truly has no clothes on! On a national or global level we seem to be impotent, but when it comes to the individual kids we work with, we aren't so impotent; we can make a difference.

## Using becomes the Problem

### Four Types of Using and Drinking

There are four types of chemical use that we will examine. These are not necessarily stages; some never go beyond the point of experimentation or seeking the mood swing. Others definitely do. The four categories are:

1. **Experimentation**—initial use; learning what it does
2. **Seeking the Mood Swing**—choosing to use because of enjoyment
3. **Harmful Involvement**—continuing to use in spite of concurring problems
4. **Chemical Dependency**—using to feel normal or to function

### It is Not Just Physical

### Continuum of Feelings

Pain                              Okay                              Pleasure

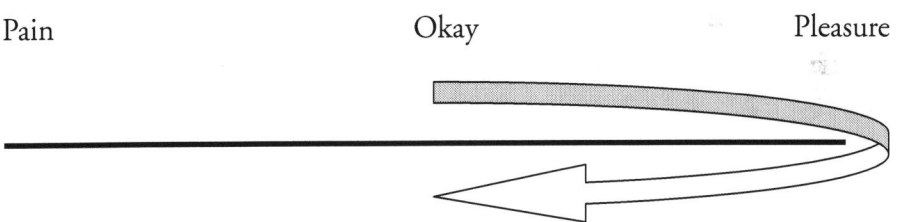

The line represents a continuum of feelings or senses. On one end is pain (guilt, remorse) and the other is pleasure (buzz, high). The arrow indicates the alcohol or drug use. The middle spot represents feeling normal or typical; not great, but not bad. For example, a person feels okay, gets high and when it wears off returns to an okay place.

# 1. Experimentation (learning about the mood swing)

Pain              Okay             Pleasure

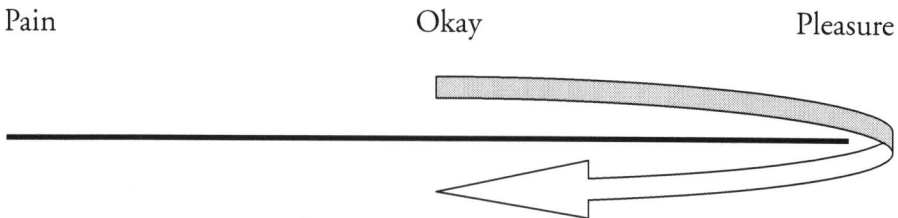

***Use results in pleasure for most and when over, teen usually returns to the emotional place prior to use.***

The first phase, *experimentation*, is short lived. In it, the individual learns what the experience of using a particular chemical is like. Once the student knows what to expect, he or she either progresses to the next category, or stops using. This shift is not always a conscious decision.

Students experiment because of curiosity, peer pressure, defiance, imitation of behaviors exhibited by role models, and a need for rites of passage to adulthood. Initial use is not to escape reality; how would one know the effects of using prior to using? While still experimentation, significant behavioral changes probably will not be noticed at school (unless it takes place before or during school hours). Scholastic problems and other negative consequences due to alcohol or other drug use are rare in this category. On the contrary, there is at times an increase in popularity. So far, the pleasure of using outweighs the pain of any consequences.

National surveys suggest between 50-80 percent of high school seniors have experimented with drugs other than alcohol. When alcohol is included, these figures increase to 97 percent. Most students who try drugs are not going to become dependent. Don't misinterpret this statement; it means that not every kid who drinks will become alcoholic. Dependency and problem use are not necessarily the same thing. However, adolescents experience problems with chemicals at about three times the norm than adults, and the younger a person is when he or she starts, the quicker a problem will occur. There is a myth that the younger one starts using, the higher the frequency of the disease. This is not true, but we do see an increase in the frequency of kids who become harmfully involved which is not dependency. No one who enters the experimentation phase plans to become chemically dependent. It is not a matter of intelligence or will power that saves a person from developing problems, but a combination of factors. One thing to remember is that if a student indicates to you that he or she has been experimenting with a substance for an extended period of time, he or she is minimizing considerably. Experimentation is short-lived in nature and either progresses, or stops. Students who are experimenting still have control over the decision to use or not use. They can respond to prevention efforts and are appropriate for strategies such as drug education and support groups. Prevention of further use and reducing harm targets a large population of students. Because someone has started to use doesn't mean she can't change her mind and stop; she just might need support. If the student continues, the use shifts to the next category. Please note that this model is based on a student being in an "okay" emotional place prior to the use. But, what about a kid who chooses to use who is already experiencing emotional pain?

*"I'm told that getting high will hurt me; it will mess up my future. Well, what if I told you getting high was my relief? What if I told you I don't care about my future? What then?"*
**Chemically Involved Youth**

## What if Already Wounded?

In almost every public service announcement, in-service or government-funded pamphlet, students are portrayed as "typical adolescents" prior to use. It is as if the playing field is level and one size fits all. What about students who are depressed before the first time they use? When encumbered with trauma, it seems that prior to using, the state of mind is "pain" and using alcohols or chemicals temporarily brings relief. It would be wonderful if everyone was in his/her normal state of mind, but this isn't the case. Different from the other examples of this continuum, pleasure or euphoria is removed to illustrate first time use by a depressed student might result in an appearance of functioning better, acting more alert and demonstrating higher self esteem. For a short time, chemical use can relieve depression, or mollify the impact of trauma. The relief is short-term and eventually stops working as well. It seems somehow illogical to give all kids the same prevention message when all kids are not the same. Threats work with some (not many), education reaches others and fear might impact a couple. With some kids, no amount of threats, education lessons, or fear will deter use. For them, life may already be painful and the attitude of "it can't get any worse" prevails. How do you reach this type of kid?

## Using When I Already feel Like Hell

More Pain                           Pain                          Relief

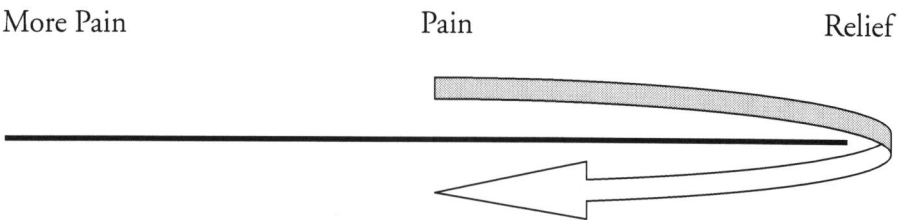

Using may enable some students to feel okay instead of feeling emotional pain. Getting high or drunk does temporarily ease the hurt. When drug wears off, kids goes back to the state of pain before the use.

## 2. Seeking the mood swing

Pain                               Okay                        Pleasure

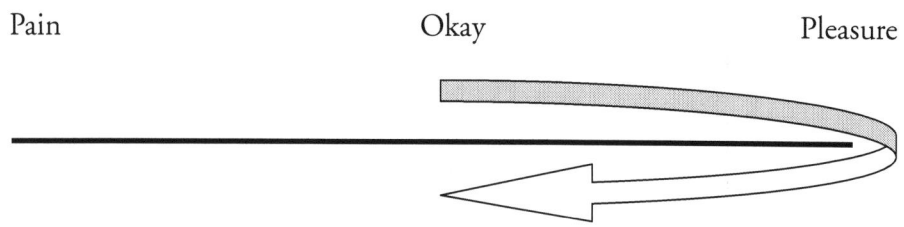

*Use continues to provide pleasure, and when the high is over, the person usually returns to the same emotional state prior to use.*

From the observer's point of view, *seeking the mood swing* looks very similar to experimentation—behavioral indicators of chemical use are still not strongly present in the school setting. Few emotionally painful consequences are experienced resulting from the use of alcohol and other drugs. Grades, family relationships, peer relationships, and self-worth are not adversely affected to a large degree. Any negative changes that begin to evolve as the result of the use are easily justified as something else, and chemical use is not a high priority. Kids who are seeking the mood swing don't exhibit many of the "warnings" they've heard about for years in prevention sessions. Subsequently, it feeds the ability to rationalize, minimize and deny any problems that do happen to come up. Instead of the drinking or drugging, problems are caused by "mom, dad, school, coach, boy or girl friend, work, etc." This suggests to them that they are "different than most", in control of use, and that using will not hurt them. For some people, the relationship with the drug of choice becomes more important and negative consequences are more apparent. When this happens, the person is in the third category which is harmful involvement.

In observing a student's behavior, it is very difficult to distinguish between harmful involvement and dependency. As an educator, one does not need to identify or diagnose what kind of drinking or drugging is being displayed in order to intervene. If the signs and symptoms interfere with learning and cannot be modified through customary classroom management techniques, then a referral to the Student Assistance Program or early intervention team is appropriate. Classroom teachers cannot be held responsible for the diagnosis and treatment of kids who are harmfully involved. This is why the Student Assistance Program is offered to schools.

### 3. Harmful Involvement

Pain                              Normal                              Pleasure

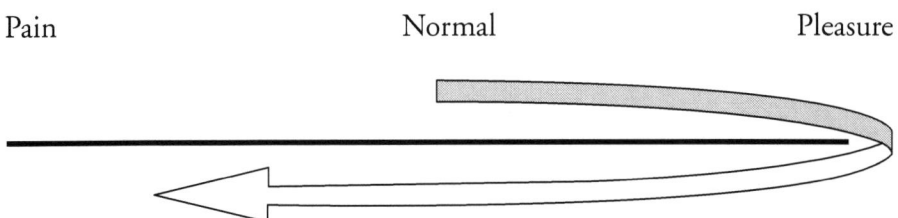

Students who are *harmfully involved* with alcohol or other drugs are experiencing emotional pain as the result of the use. It becomes more important on the priority list. Getting high or drunk temporarily provides relief. When the high is over, the person's emotional state resorts back to restlessness or discontent. The alcohol or other drug use meets such needs that he or she is willing to pay a high price to continue using. Behaviors presented include defiance, withdrawal, anger, poor school performance, quitting hobbies and activities that were once important, endorsement of drug and alcohol use, and inability to complete tasks.

Another behavior seen is a change in peers. Adolescents have a tendency toward peer clustering. This dynamic is referenced by the phrase, "Birds of a feather flock together". Adolescents are more comfortable around others who behave similarly (we all are). Rarely will a student hang out around users unless he or she is using. This helps explain why young people who begin using significant amounts of alcohol and other drugs often change their circle of friends, unless others in the circle also use.

By far, there are more kids who are *harmfully involved* than are *chemically dependent*. Data suggests that of those who use alcohol or other drugs, between five and fifteen percent become chemically dependent. Up to forty percent of teenagers who use become *harmfully involved*. There are those whose use does not appear to create problems, much like adults who socially drink. But, the use is not social; it is usually to get drunk, buzzed or blown away—therefore it shouldn't be termed social drinking.

Though *harmful involvement* is not the disease, the student may need professional help to stop. The use meets needs that are such that quitting may be either difficult or considered impossible. Consequences continue to occur with most that are in this category, including decreased grades, poor attendance, patterns of behavior changes and significant mood swings. It isn't difficult to tell when a student is experiencing a problem to this extent. Just observe and pay attention. Because of genetic and environmental factors, a small percent of these students cross this invisible line into dependency. Genetics loads the gun and the environment pulls the trigger. There may be shades of gray in this crossing, but when it has happened, there rarely is the ability to reverse the amount or frequency of use; these students have become *chemically dependent* and are using to feel normal.

> *"First the man takes the drink; then the drink takes the drink; finally the drink takes the man."*
> **Chinese Proverb**

## When Choice is Gone

Once a person crosses into *chemical dependency*, evidence does not support the claim that people can "undo" their dependency. Trials and research have been seeking proof that an alcoholic can be made a social drinker. To date,

I know of none that were successful. Over the years these attempts have included the use of LSD, electric shock, induced vomiting, psychoanalysis, deprivation and rewards. None of these worked or we would right now be able to cure dependency rather than treat it. True recovery requires total abstinence if a person has the disease of chemical dependency. If only about 10% of kids who use become dependent, it implies a large number who are harmfully involved will "outgrow" the problem as they mature and take on responsibilities. What makes this awkward is that it is very difficult to know which kids will outgrow the problem and which ones will struggle for a lifetime (unless he or she lives sober).

### 4. Chemical Dependency (using to feel normal)

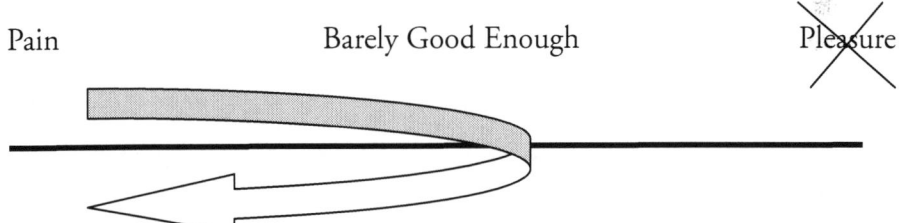

Pain                      Barely Good Enough                      Pleasure

*The use takes the person out of the emotional pain, but when the high is over he or she returns to the emotional pain. That which is the problem is seen as the solution.*

In this phase, there is little chance that someone will outgrow the problem. Dependency has occurred, negative consequences abound, and no amount of pleading, threatening, or bribing will reduce it. This *chemical dependency* may or may not include physical addiction. It always seems to include psychological addiction. Expecting a student who is chemically dependent to simply say no is like asking someone with tuberculosis to simply stop coughing. Help is needed. The following is known and understood about *chemical dependency*: it is a chronic disease. Once an individual has this disease, there is no reversing it. In addition, there is a progressive nature that dictates a predictable pattern of use and harmful consequences. The behaviors exhibited are intensified or compounded. Guilt and other emotional conflicts increase, caused by the violation of values and morals. Self-dislike begins to be projected out toward others, resulting in anger, distance and rebellion. This further reinforces the self-perception of being bad and feeling worthless.

There was a time that a mainstream student hid his or her drug use from peers out of concern they would disapprove. Today, it isn't a surprise when a similar student tells us that drug use is different. There is no pressure to hide cannabis use. It is part of the "party" environment. As much as this statement is true, there are many exceptions. Not all mainstream kids use pot and not all parties include it as part of the entertainment.

> *"Genetics loads the gun; then the environment pulls the trigger."*
> **Dr. Carlton Erickson**

## Difference between Misuse and Dependency

Misuse and chemical dependency are not the same thing. According to *the Diagnostic and Statistical Manual IV,* the publication used to diagnose mental health issues:

**It is misuse or abuse when one or two of the indicators below occur within twelve-month period.**
1. Recurrent use leading to failure to fulfill major obligations
2. Recurrent use which is physically hazardous
3. Recurrent drug-related legal problems
4. Continued use despite social or interpersonal problems

**It is the disease of chemical dependency when three or more of the indicators below occur in a twelve-month period.**
1. Tolerance
2. Withdrawal
3. Taken in larger amounts or over longer periods of time than intended
4. Persistent desire or failed effort to cut down or control use
5. Great deal of time spent on obtaining and using the substance
6. Important social, educational, occupational or recreational activities given up or reduced
7. Use continues in spite of having knowledge of harmful effects

As defenses (rationalization, minimization, denial, projection, etc.) form to protect the individual from the emotional pain resulting from destructive alcohol or other drug use, a person builds a wall, cutting him self off from the assistance most desperately needed. The more important the alcohol or other drug use becomes to the person's sense of survival, the more this person will protect and hide his or her use. For students in the first two categories, education and family boundaries can be very beneficial. Once a student has become harmfully involved, some structured help is needed. By the time dependency is evident twelve step programs and/or treatment is often necessary and sometimes the only things that will work. A person cannot be too young to get sober. A person does not have to hit bottom and lose everything to desire recovery. You cannot lead a horse to water and make it drink. But, you can show it where the water is and make it thirsty!

All of the information presented on the topic of chemical dependency also applies to adults. The primary difference is that by adulthood most people who are harmfully involved change their behavior or patterns of use. Think about the kid you knew in school who was constantly stoned, yet is now a well functioning, non-drug dependent adult. If an adult is still drinking or using in a problematic way, it more likely is chemical dependency. With the disease, no amount of responsibility or growing up will help. DNA has a great deal to do with who is and is not chemically dependent. Having an alcoholic parent increases the odds of becoming chemically dependent 40% over someone who doesn't have an alcoholic parent. When both mom and dad are alcoholic, it increases to 70%. Another contributing factor is a person's family tree. Just like dominant and recessive genes for eye color or left-handedness can skip a generation, so do genes for dependency. Mom and dad may not have inherited the gene, but Junior has.

# Testing Your Knowledge
True or False

1.  Teenagers develop chemical dependency at higher rates than adults

    **T   F**

2.  Chemically dependent teenagers can appear as if everything is normal

    **T   F**

3.  Drugs have equal addiction potential

    **T   F**

4.  Less than 20% of people who use cocaine become addicted

    **T   F**

5.  Marijuana can cause an overdose death

    **T   F**

6.  Addiction is a will power issue

    **T   F**

7.  Knowledge of chemical dependency allows one to use in a "safer" manner

    **T   F**

8.  Not all drugs damage brain cells

    **T   F**

9.  The younger a person starts drinking the more prone to alcoholism

    **T   F**

10. Girls become intoxicated faster than boys

    **T   F**

11. One 12 oz. beer equals 4 oz. of wine and 1 ½ oz. of 80% liquor

    **T   F**

12. Alcohol is one of the most toxic of all mood altering chemicals

    **T   F**

13. Inhalant use causes brain or organ damage

    T  F

14. Blackouts are good indicators of alcoholism

    T  F

15. The brain has specific receptor sites for marijuana

    T  F

16. The brain has specific receptor sites for alcohol

    T  F

17. Alcohol use kills 6 ½ times as many youth as all the other drugs combined

    T  F

18. Dependency is the same thing as physical addiction

    T  F

19. Withdrawal always indicates dependency

    T  F

20. Addiction is a behavioral problem

    T  F

21. There is no cure of chemical dependency

    T  F

# Answers

1. **Teenagers develop chemical dependency at higher rates than adults**
   **False**
   The younger a person starts using the faster the problem will develop. Chemical dependency is more a result of genetically shared bio-chemical predisposition. A person is born with the bio-chemical makeup for dependency. It does not occur because of age.

2. **Chemically dependent teenagers can appear as if everything is normal**
   **True**
   Some students can maintain grades and continue behaving in an appropriate manner when chemically dependent. Not all demonstrate the stereotypical problems that bring troubled kids to our attention. This does not mean that everything is ok.

3. **Drugs have equal addiction potential**
   **False**
   There are drugs like heroin and cocaine that result in a higher rate of dependency (17%) than marijuana and alcohol (8%-11%).

4. **Less than 20% of people who use crack and meth become addicted**
   **True**
   Contrary to popular belief, approximately 17% of crack and meth users become chemically dependency. Misuse by anyone can create significant problems, even if not dependency

5. **Marijuana can cause an overdose death**
   **False**
   The properties of marijuana do not cause physical death. A person cannot "smoke themselves to death."

6. **Addiction is a will power issue**
   **False**
   Once addicted a person has a compulsion and obsession to use that is partly caused by bio-chemical. Many people who are chemically dependent demonstrate strong will power in other areas of their life not controlled by the dependency.

7. **Knowledge of chemical dependency allows one to use in a "safer" manner**                                **False**

   Information alone does not prevent dependency. Many people with a tremendous knowledge of this disease (physicians, pharmacist, counselors) still become dependent.

8. **Not all drugs damage brain cells**                                **True**

   Contrary to popular belief, very few of the drugs commonly used in our society do permanent physical damage to the brain. Research shows that even when a drug produces a physical change in the brain (ecstasy), the brain returns to its usual state.

9. **The younger a person starts drinking the more prone to alcoholism**
   **False**

   People who begin using or drinking at an early age tend to develop the disease faster than those who wait until 21. Age doesn't seem to be one of the factors in whether people get this disease or not. A young age does increase the frequency of abuse or misuse.

10. **Girls become intoxicated faster than boys**                                **True**

    This has more to do with how females metabolize alcohol than weight. Weight does have an impact on intoxication, but girls who weigh the same as a boy still get intoxicated faster.

11. **One 12 oz. beer equals 4 oz. of wine and 1 ½ oz. of 80% liquor**
    **True**

    Claiming "it's just beer" is not a valid justification for drinking. It is the alcohol in the beer, wine and liquor that is intoxicating. Beer does provide more liquid to dilute the alcohol, but does not diminish the amount. People tend to drink more beer than hard liquor. This is a generalization with recognized exceptions.

12. **Alcohol is one of the most toxic of all mood altering chemicals**
    **True**

    Alcohol has a damaging impact on the internal organs much more than the "street drugs". A few of the drugs are very toxic, but alcohol rates high on the danger list. There are certain drugs that are considered more "benign"; alcohol is not one of them.

13. **Inhalant use causes brain or organ damage**                    **True**
    This is chemical use that is extremely toxic and can do damage with
    first time use. There are many products in the inhalant category. There
    are none that are safe to use.

14. **Blackouts are good indicators of alcoholism**                  **False**
    Even though many alcoholics experience this chemically induced
    amnesia, blackouts can occur with heavy drinking with non-alcoholics.
    They are not a good diagnostic tool to determine chemical dependency.
    Blackouts do indicate misuse or abuse of alcohol.

15. **The brain has specific receptor sites for marijuana**           **True**
    Research is showing that our brains have more than 400 receptor sites.
    Why this includes endocanibinoids is still unknown. Receptor sites
    indicate that our brains produce miniscule amounts of chemicals for
    normal reasons that are molecularly similar to drugs of abuse.

16. **The brain has specific receptor sites for alcohol**             **False**
    Researchers refer to alcohol as the "dirty drug" because instead of
    binding to a specific receptor site, it tends to disperse and impact
    whatever part of the brain it can reach.

17. **Alcohol use kills 6 ½ times as many youth as all the other drugs
    combined**                                                         **True**
    An obvious reason is because much more alcohol is consumed by
    teenagers than the other drugs. But, by far the most popular drug used
    (marijuana) does not have a fatal point of consumption. Alcohol not
    only poses a physical risk, but often leads to behavior that is very risky
    (inhibitions are lessened).

18. **Dependency is the same thing as physical addiction**            **False**
    Everyone can become physically addicted to opiates such as morphine;
    it is a phenomenon that occurs at a cellular level. Approximately
    15%-20% of those who use the drug will become chemically dependent
    which includes physical addiction. But, it also includes many more
    indicators. A person with chronic pain requiring medication will often
    become physically dependent, yet not show any other indicators of the
    disease.

19. **Withdrawal always indicates dependency**                **False**

This point can be made by referencing caffeine. People who stop drinking coffee after a long period experience withdrawal symptoms. None of the other indicators exist.

20. **Addiction is a behavioral problem**                **False**

Addiction without a doubt can cause behavioral problems. It is not a behavioral problem in the sense that behavior or cognitive therapy is unsuccessful in treating it. Dependency and addiction occur at the cellular level and manifest with an obsession and compulsion to drink or drug.

21. **There is no cure of chemical dependency**                **True**

So far, medicine and science have not been able to discover a way to actually cure chemical dependency. By using the word "cure", we are talking about the disease being completely gone and no longer affecting a person. People do recover from this disease and are able to arrest the use. But, the ability to drink or drug again in a non-dependent fashion is non-existent. Any use triggers the disease (even when dormant) and the obsession and compulsion return, often in a more destructive manner.

University of Texas Addiction Science and Research Center

*"Up on Cripple Creek she sends me; If I spring a leak she mends me*
*I don't have to speak, she defends me; A drunkard's dream if I ever did see one."*
**Cripple Creek, The Band**

# Chapter 11

# Don't Let Me Fall

Deception for Protection

## Enabling

*Enabling* is protecting another person from the natural consequences of his or her behavior, because it somehow meets the protector's needs. We tend to *enable* those we like. This definition covers a lot of territory and includes most of us at some point. Rare is the adult who has never protected a young person from his or her own mistakes. *Enabling* can take the shape of ignoring a problem, making excuses, blaming, minimizing, or rationalizing. As educators, *enabling* shows up in many forms. Helping a student avoid consequences that result from his or her behavior is *enabling*. Justifying behaviors or even condemning a student is also considered *enabling*. *Enabling* occurs when a teacher takes responsibility for a student's behavior or when the teacher is inconsistent in the classroom. Parents enable by making excuses for their children's inappropriate behavior or bailing them out of trouble. A typical form of *enabling* is when a parent writes an excuse for truancy just to keep the student from getting in trouble. Professional counselors and therapists enable when they misdiagnose or "take on" the client's pain and conflict. The key to reducing *enabling* is to understand that when we enable, the problem only gets worse. As long as we protect people from natural consequences, there is no reason for them to make changes. *Enabling* is not confused with coming to the aid of someone who is the victim of circumstances. The Good Samaritan was not an enabler.

## Examples of Enabling in School

Manipulating students to get appropriate behavior
Assuming that "it isn't my problem"
Making empty threats
Ignoring the problem
Waiting and doing nothing
Blaming parents
Justifying poor performance
Excusing poor attendance
Lowering expectations
Moralizing

*"The worst lies are the lies we tell ourselves. We live in denial of what we do, even what we think. We do this because we're afraid."*
*Richard Bach*

## Denial

It has been said that the last person to know he has a problem with alcohol is the alcoholic. This applies to a number of other problems. Denial is powerful and effective. Quite often, it takes "hitting bottom" in order to break through denial. Until denial is addressed, a person can easily remain deluded into seeing things the way he/she wants to see them.

## After the Fact

Mr. Love, would you please step into my office? There were a whole lot of words I had rather heard than these. The person making the request was my high school assistant principal, and most of what he did at school involved discipline. As far as we knew, discipline was what he did all day, every day. We did not see him in any other light. This perception was about to change; but, that change would not come for six years.

At the age of sixteen, my first reaction to Mr. Vernon's request was to quickly do a back scan and figure out what it was that got me in trouble. I really thought I'd gotten away with everything. This would be one time, in retrospect, I wish I had not gotten away with. With a hesitant shuffle and downcast frown, I entered his office and took a seat.

Initially, Mr. Vernon engaged in small talk. Then asked how things were going at school. He asked if I had a girlfriend and what I thought of the University of Texas football team. I answered in a casual way, trying to look innocent of whatever it was he was about to slam me with. I could not have been more wrong.

The office got quiet; it was almost hushed. Mr. Vernon looked at me with a strange expression and asked me one more question, prefaced by a comment. He said; *"Noel, I know things aren't going very well at home and I wanted to know if you were interested in talking about it?"* His question perplexed me. I sat and thought about it and eventually responded by saying, *"I don't know what you are talking about."*

I said no more and just sat looking around his office, hoping for a good distraction. Before looking away, I saw a sad look on his face that registered resignation; he had not gotten through to me. I distinctly recall not knowing what he was talking about. I wasn't avoiding anything. I certainly wasn't being dishonest or evasive. Well, at least to Mr. Vernon I wasn't.

To illustrate the point of this story, we need to leave school and enter the front door to my house. Inside were five other kids, ranging from sixteen to six, my brothers and sisters. Over the last several years, we witnessed a slow-motion destruction of our family as we knew it. Left were bits and pieces of those things all kids should embrace: hope, excitement, wonder, safety, calm and trust. I understand as an adult that twenty-four percent of our students live in a home devastated by some form of addiction. That might have been statistically accurate even back then, but all I knew it was my family's world that had been turned upside down.

For several years, my father had served on the city council and had a very visible position running a local television station. Prior to that, he had been a sports caster at 6:00 pm and 10:00 pm. He was well known. While growing up, I got used to hearing others remark on what a cool dad I had. I would smile, nod my head and let the comment fall flat on the ground. I did not want to talk badly about my dad, so I gave no response.

Being the oldest of six, I was keenly aware of the trouble in my family. A day did not go by when some aspect of the loss did not present itself. My father moved out, resigned from the council and generally dropped out of our lives. None of this is written in anger or with resentment; my father has been sober more than thirty-five years and I am proud to call him my father. But, as a sixteen year old high school student who was invested in trying to make the family look better, Mr. Vernon's attempt fell flat.

The most striking aspect of this situation was my sincere inability to tie my father's alcoholism to Mr. Vernon's kind effort. When he asked if I wanted some help, I simply could not make the connection. It was like looking straight at my hand and declaring; "what hand?" Looking back I wish that I would have been responsive; I certainly needed to talk to someone.

Five years later, while working as an alcoholism counselor in the Air Force, I was doing a lecture series on how the family is damaged by the disease. From out of nowhere came the revelation; "he was talking about dad's drinking!" I had not been thinking about Mr. Vernon, high school or even my dad's drinking. Why it popped up at that time is a mystery to me. I called my old high school assistant principal and asked him if he remembered that day. He said he did. I told him that I had just gotten it; I just realized what he was talking about back then. With a tight throat and misty eyes I thanked him for what he tried to do. I told him that it took five years to sink in, but I finally got it. Talk about a slow learner.

Denial is not the refusal to see things clearly; this is *minimization*. *Denial* is the *inability* to see things as they really are. Denial serves a purpose. It serves as armor for protection against painful situations. The closer one is to the situation, the more the *denial*. Parents often experience *denial* as much, or more than their children do. Educators, including teachers and administrators experience *denial*, particularly if what is occurring replicates their earlier personal experiences.

When a person experiences *denial*, he or she is not aware of it. Instead of recognizing exactly what the problem is, he or she avoids addressing the issue—focusing instead on peripheral distractions. *Denial* can exist even when one is faced with overwhelming evidence that something is wrong. *Denial* is experienced in individuals, families, work places, schools, communities, and nations. Unless challenged, *denial* prevents change. *Denial* can obscure perception and accountability.

## Statements that often indicate denial

> Not my kid; no way.
> She was fine until she met that boy.
> He told me it wasn't his. What a relief.
> No son of mine would ever do that.

*Denial* can be reversed by a crisis that is significant enough to shatter the illusion that things are ok. This crisis can be a natural consequence or manufactured. The benefit of a manufactured crisis is that it can be done before things get too bad, and in a manner that prevents a tremendous amount of wreckage. Naturally occurring crisis on the other hand include automobile accidents, emergency hospital visits, expulsion from school or suicide attempt.

I once did a behavioral health assessment on a high school girl who had made some vague comments about death in one of her classrooms. The parents were called and I ended up seeing all three; both separately and together. While alone with me the young lady told me that twice she picked up her father's pistol, put it to her head with the intension of shooting herself. She wasn't sure why she changed her mind either time. When I told her I could not keep that information secret and that her parents needed to know, she said; "go ahead and tell them, they won't care anyway."

I told both parents about the incidents with the pistol and they announced that it would be taken care of at home. When I asked how, they told me that they would nail her window to her bedroom shut, remove the door off its hinges, take her phone away and ground her. I looked at them trying to hide my sense of incredulity and repeated my question; "how will you deal with her suicidal impulses at home?" When they did not offer any more strategies, I informed the mother and father that I would contact child protective services and report neglect. Their response to that was to ask if I really thought it was that big of a deal.

On another occasion, I was providing a similar behavioral health assessment on a fourteen-year-old boy. While speaking with his parents privately, they informed me that they found a cigar box under his bed with empty vials and a syringe. When they confronted him, he explained that "it belongs to a friend". I asked if they believed him and they told me they did and made a deal with their son. If he no longer associated with that friend, they would buy him a brand new motorcycle. There was direct evidence of serious, life threatening drug use in his room and he gets a new motorcycle. It wasn't a lack of love, but more a need to pretend the problem did not exist. What is sad is that what may wake the parents up is a phone call from the police about an accident on some dark winding road. This is how *denial* presents itself. Not looking at the truth because it either hurts too much or requires an action that is strongly resisted. Once the pain of the situation exceeds any sense of comfort or safety, then people will act.

# Minimizing

*Minimizing* is making less of something through justification, denial, isolation, withdrawal or excuses. Whereas denial is the inability to see the truth, when *minimizing*, a person sees it and does what he or she can to make it less so. It is quite natural for parents to initially *minimize* problems their children are experiencing. It is even more natural for the person who has the problem to *minimize* the situation.

**Some statements by parents and students that tend to minimize a problem include:**

*"I don't care!"*
*"You are exaggerating!"*
*"Come on, it isn't that bad!"*
*"Let's hope he outgrows it!"*
*"I haven't been locked up yet!"*
*"It's only money; it could have been worse!"*
*"I see others who are a lot worse than I am!"*
*"He just drinks; thank God he isn't doing drugs!"*
*"Honey, maybe it is a fad and he will grow out of it."*
*"I did the same when I was young; I turned out ok!"*

# Doing the Defense Dance

*"Behavior in the human being is sometimes a defense, a way of concealing motives and thought as language can be a way of hiding your thoughts and preventing communication."*
**Abraham Maslow**

In order to avoid some of the more profound or painful realizations and feelings, people use a wide variety of defense mechanisms, with *denial* and *minimizing* being only two of them. The following list is an abbreviated list that originally was too long for this book.

- **Anger** tends to push people away. The best defense is a good offense.
- **Blame** is laying the judgment for your problems upon someone else.
- **Compliance** is giving in to the wishes of another to avoid confrontation.
- **Defiance** is daring others to prove that you are wrong.
- **Displacement** is the transferring of a strong emotion from the real issue to a safer or more acceptable substitute.
- **Excuse** is the use of logic that may appear to be acceptable to avoid an issue.
- **Humor** is making a joke out of a grave or hurtful situation.
- **Intellectualization** is the avoidance of conflicts by the excessive use of an intellectual guise of words, thoughts, or debate.
- **Being judgmental** is placing others on a lower level to cover one's own inadequacies.
- **Justification** is trying to balance your wrong with the wrong of others.
- **Manipulation** is indirectly influencing others to comply with your desires without them being aware of it.
- **Questioning** is firing questions at the person to keep him or her from bringing up threatening issues in your own life.
- **Rationalization** is a way to avoid facing responsibility by coming up with good excuses.
- **Regression** is the reverting to an earlier age of development.
- **Repression** is the involuntary exclusion of unwanted thoughts or feelings from the individual's consciousness.
- **Somatization** is the unconscious shifting of a strong negative emotion into physical symptoms such as pain.
- **Threatening** is using aggression to avoid facing an issue.
- **Withdrawing** is deliberate removal of one's self from the situation.

## Building Bricks in a Fortress

*"I have my walls, a fortress deep and mighty, that none may penetrate.*
*I have no need of friendship; friendship causes pain, its' laughter and its' loving*
*I disdain. I am a rock, I am an island."*
### I am a Rock, Simon and Garfunkel,

Below are some common phrases that serve as protection against seeing things as they truly are. Using these "bricks" as building material, one can erect a fortress to hide within or keep others out.

*"Everyone does it."*
*"I am just human."*
*"Leave me alone!"*
*"They made me do it."*
*"It's your entire fault."*
*"Can't you take a laugh?"*
*"Well, no one is perfect."*
*"It wasn't all that important."*
*"It was just a little white lie."*
*"I don't want to talk about it!"*
*"There was no other way out."*
*"I just needed a pick-me-up."*
*"I say, if it feels right, do it."*
*"I just lost temporary control."*
*"Who is it to say that I am wrong?"*
*"It was just a practical joke, O.K.?"*
*"They deserved what I did to them."*
*"It was only a one time experience."*
*"You just need to get with the times."*
*"Well, it happened a long time ago."*
*"He / she does not deserve forgiveness."*
*"You just don't understand my situation."*
*"I couldn't help it; I was having a bad day."*
*"I can't help it. My parents were that way."*
*"I have the right to do anything that I want."*
*"Somebody needed to put them in their place."*
*"My opinion is just as good as the next person."*
*"Everyone needs to let off a little steam sometimes."*
*"Why should I suffer while they can do what they want?"*
*"I don't have a problem. You are the one with the problem."*

Having some understanding of these issues enhances the ability to deal with them. It would be a huge mistake to leave it at that and move on to the next section without acknowledging the fact that all students possess strengths that can be recognized. Over the last several decades, much has gone into understanding why some students appear more resilient than others, even when problems exist in their lives. Educators are in an excellent position to foster this resiliency and build upon the strengths that students have, even when they are hard to spot.

## The Sorrow Tree

### An Old Hassidic Parable

On judgment day, God told all the people that they could take their sorrows and pain and hang them on a tree. His one condition is that they had to put all of their sorrows on the tree, and then pick up someone else's sorrow. At first, the people rejoiced, danced and praised Him. Surely, each could find someone else's sorrow and pain. For each of the people thought their own sorrow was unique and arduous, as if no one else had it so bad.

With excitement and anticipation, the people took their pain and sorrow, hung it on the tree and began the search. They searched high and low, gave considerable thought to other people's burdens, and even tried on a few for size. The people walked in circles around this tree finding that the only sorrow and pain that fit was their own. With resignation and a newfound awareness, the people realized that the pain and sorrow experienced in life were part of what made them who they are. As much as it hurt, the growth and wisdom that came from the experiences was evident.

With a renewed sense of understanding of His purpose, the people took back their pain and sorrow, recognizing and accepting that pain and suffering, like joy and comfort, were part of being human. The people no longer wondered why they had to suffer. They no longer questioned misfortune. They learned that some of the greatest blessings of all come disguised as tragedy and despair. They learned that everything that happened to them, good and bad, was part of their life-story, and could not be ignored or eliminated.

The moral of the story is strength and perseverance are spawned by adversity. Muscle unused atrophies; muscle used strengthens. The sorrow and pain experienced in life had much to do with forming character and fortitude.

*"Resiliency is bouncing back from problems and
stuff with more power and more smarts."*
**15 Year-Old Student**

# Chapter 12

# To Survive Anyway

## Why some do well anyway!

Why is it some students seem to weather the storms of life better than others? How can we explain the student who has every reason in the world to give up and he or she actually seems to thrive? In the midst of dysfunction, insanity, violence, fear, dishonesty, abandonment, and the unknown, the student has resiliency that results in growth even without the sunshine.

Is it DNA, luck or some astrological sign? Resiliency is an ability to go through difficult situations and come out on the other side with strength and resolve. It has become more apparent that most people, including students, can recover from trauma and other difficult life experiences.

Resiliency is built when one has a relationship with another adult who is trustworthy, consistent, affirming and nurturing. Resiliency is not a "magic suit" that protects a child from the damage of the situation. It doesn't stop the hurt or wounding. It does impact how the child develops in the future.

Prior to our industrial revolution, the average person lived in a society of about 150 people or less. Small towns, villages, and farms made up a child's world. It really does take a village to raise children. We have lost what for centuries was a norm. We went from knowing almost everyone we saw, to avoiding eye contact on the sidewalk. People close their eyes when someone else's child needs a reprimand, taking false comfort in the delusion that, "it isn't my kid, it's none of my business!" Today, research has offered some good news regarding children receiving what is essential from family and society. Resiliency is not an accident. It can be premeditated, planned and labored over. It can also happen for reasons not apparent. This next section examines some of this research and presents information that should be helpful in classroom management and can be utilized in the entire school and even community.

## Search Institute's Developmental Assets

Based on a study of more than 250,000 children, aged 12-18, the Search Institute identified forty positive experiences and qualities that all of us have the power to bring into the lives of children and youth, which are called *developmental assets*. These assets are essential to growing up as competent and caring adults. Research shows an astounding correlation between the number of assets possessed by a child and the likelihood of being successful (or avoiding major problems). Of these forty assets, twenty are considered internal (qualities the person has) and twenty are external (positive experiences provided by surrounding family, community, school, etc.).

## Of the Forty . . .

**The average child in our society possesses less than half of these developmental assets.**
**Girls have an average of 20.7.**
**Boys possess an average of 17.8 assets.**
**Sixth graders possess more assets than older teenagers, 23.1 compared to 18.3.**

We inherently understand that if our culture were more adept at building these developmental assets, there would be less of a need for the extraordinary efforts put forth in programs such as the Student Assistance Program. Unfortunately, we are a long way from adequately building these assets to that degree. Instead, it is our responsibility to promote the concept of developmental assets in our families, campuses and communities. By connecting students to support services, we are building these assets. By helping students get into treatment for chemical dependency, we are helping to eliminate the road blocks to building these assets. By simply calling a quiet and shy student by his or her first name builds assets. All students need these assets and the school is an effective environment for fostering the identification, cultivation, and harvesting of a number of asset building strategies that reach the entire student body. Below, is a list of external and internal assets. Be cognizant that assets are not "rocket science" and are intuitive and fostered by a common sense approach. Educators have been building assets for years without knowing the language. Instead of the process of building assets being accidental, it needs to be intentional.

*"Our greatest glory is not in never failing, but in rising every time we fail."*
**Kung Fu-tzu Confucius**

## Twenty External Assets

Provided by family, school, community and culture.

### Support—how important does the child feel?
√ Family Support—family life provides high level of love and support.
√ Positive family communication—young person and his or her parent(s) communicate.
√ Other adult relationships—young person receives support from three or more non parent adults.
√ Caring neighborhood—young person experiences caring neighbors.
√ Caring school climate—school provides a caring, encouraging environment.
√ Parent involvement in schooling—parent(s) are actively involved in helping young person.

## Empowerment—is the child treated as valuable?

√ Community values youth—young person perceives that adults in the community value youth.

√ Youth as resource—young people are given useful roles in the community.

√ Service to others—young person serves in the community one hour or more per week.

√ Safety—young person feels safe at home, at school, and in the neighborhood.

## Boundaries and Expectations—are there rules and standards for the child?

√ Family boundaries—family has clear rules and consequences and monitors young person.

√ School boundaries—school provides clear rules and consequences.

√ Neighborhood boundaries—neighbor takes responsibility for protecting young people.

√ Adult role models—parent(s) and other adults model positive, responsible behavior.

√ Positive peer influence—young person's best friends' model responsible behavior.

√ High expectations—parent(s) and teachers encourage the young person to do well.

## Constructive Use of Time—is time well spent?

√ Creative activities—young person spends three hours or more per week in lessons and practice.

√ Youth programs—young person spends three or more hours per week in sports and clubs.

√ Religious programs—young person spends one or more hours per week in church activities.

√ Time at home—young person is out with friends "with nothing to do" two or fewer nights per week.

## Twenty Internal Assets

These are the attitudes and mind-set from within that are essential to resilience.

### Commitment to Learning—how does the child feel as a learner?

√ Achievement motivation—young person is motivated to do well in school.

√ School engagement—young person is actively engaged in learning.

√ Homework—young person reports doing at least one hour of homework per night.

√ Bonding to school—young person cares about his or her school.

√ Reading for pleasure—young person reads for pleasure three or more hours per week.

### Positive Values—are there basic core values in place?

√ Caring—young person places high value on helping others.

√ Equality and social justice—person places high value on promoting equality and reducing poverty.

√ Integrity—young person acts on convictions and stands up for her or his beliefs.

√ Honesty—young person "tells the truth even when it is not easy".

√ Responsibility—young person accepts and takes personal responsibility.

√ Restraint—young person believes it is important not to be sexually active or use alcohol or other drugs.

### Social Competence—how well can the child handle different situations?

√ Planning and decision making—young person knows how to plan ahead and make choices.

√ Interpersonal competence—young person has empathy, sensitivity, and friendship skills.

√ Cultural sensitivity—young person has knowledge of and comfort with people of diverse backgrounds.

√ Resistance skills—young person can resist negative peer pressure and dangerous situations.

√ Peaceful conflict resolution—young person seeks to resolve conflict nonviolently.

**Positive Identity—what kind of personal identity does this child have?**

√   Personal power—young person feels he or she has control over "things that happen to me."

√   Self-esteem—young person reports having a high self-esteem.

√   Sense of purpose—young person reports that "my life has a purpose".

√   Positive view of personal future—young person is optimistic about her or his personal future.

The percentage of kids who have particular asset changes and current data is available at *www.search-institute.org*

The correlation between the above information and student success is such that it begs parents, schools and communities to re-assess the priority a committed approach to building assets deserves. Though there are outstanding programs available, the emphasis in building assets focuses on the personal relationships that exist between students and adults. The more assets possessed by the student body, the fewer incidents of violence, alcohol or other drug use, pregnancies, drop outs and academic failures. In a best case scenario, building assets is akin to pouring a solid foundation. Once dry and secure, the rest of the structure can be built on top. Assets will strengthen existing efforts such as tutorials, content mastery, discipline management, support groups, mentoring, peer mediation and any other ongoing efforts.

> *"The strongest oak of the forest is not the one that is protected from the storm and hidden from the sun. It's the one that stands in the open where it is compelled to struggle for its existence against the winds and rains and the scorching sun."*
> *Napoleon Hill (1883-1970)*

Children with 31-40 assets show a huge increase in the ability to exhibit leadership, maintain good health, value diversity and succeed in school. The students with 0-10 assets showed a significant increase in problem alcohol and illicit drug use, violent behavior and sexual activity.

## The Gap in Assets among Youth

| | |
|---|---|
| 0-10 assets | 15% |
| 11-20 assets | 41% |
| 21-30 assets | 35% |
| 31-40 assets | 9% |

An excellent book to read is Peter Benson's **All Kids Are Our Kids** and its companion **What Kids Need to Succeed.** Both of these are offered by Free Spirit Publishing. Their address is 400 First Avenue North, #616, Minneapolis, MN 55401-1724. The phone number to the publisher is (800) 735-7323 and the web site is *www.freespirit.com.*

*When the world says, "Give up,"*
*Hope whispers, "Try it one more time."*
**~Author Unknown**

# Section 2

## Intervention Techniques and Skills

*"When written in Chinese the word "crisis" is composed of two characters—one represents danger and the other represents opportunity."*
**John F. Kennedy, address, 12 April 1959**

# Chaos for Me

I think I have forgotten my name
My age does not matter
Nor does my shell
When I look behind me
All I see is a hole

Before me, the ground is stone
My inside is too
When did that happen?
Surely, I am made of something
Vapor, maybe a mist

Eyes pass right through me
I am right here
If eyes cannot see me
Maybe my sound will find a way
My sound reaches no ears

I think I must be lost
Try to become what I am not
Another way to fail
I have to do something
Like shout, flail about or cut with tongue

Go back inside where I am safe
Back inside where you cannot see me
My vault made of thoughts
A mess for you
Chaos for me

I wish I knew how to ask for help

*"The window of opportunity for effective interventions
opens early and rarely, if ever, closes."*
**David Satcher**

# Chapter 13

# Interventions Vary

## A Disguised Gift for Michael

The phone rang. At another, better time in her life, she might have run to answer it, panicked for fear of missing that "most important" call. Maybe it would be news she had won the lottery, or had inherited millions from a long-lost relative. You know, the kind of call everyone hopes comes through one day. But that was another time in her life, for now Mrs. Miller panicked all right, but for a very different kind of fear—a fear that had been growing in her for several months. She considered not answering and pretending no one was home. Better yet, she considered getting in her car, deciding a direction and just hitting the road. No answer today. Nope, no one home. Her maternal instincts told her that this phone call was not good news. It was about her fifteen year old son, Michael. She was right as rain, bulls-eye, and dead center. You see, Mrs. Miller did not hit the road. She did not head for the setting sun; instead, she reluctantly and fearfully reached out and did what parents have had to do; she answered the phone. With a cold steel running down her back, Mrs. Miller heard the following:

Michael had been involved in an automobile accident. Amazingly-no miraculously—Michael wasn't seriously hurt. That was the only good news! You see, when the other kid was brought to the emergency room, the morgue was informed of a "probable" fatality. The probable became certain at 1:35 AM when Michael's best friend died from massive head trauma. In a one car accident, on some desolate highway, on a cold winter's night Brian Cortez was crushed as he was thrown out of a window while his car rolled over and over. The police officer's report indicated that Michael and his now belated friend, Brian, had been drinking and drugging. Brian was not wearing his seat belt that night. Michael was wearing his, but he doesn't remember buckling it.

This came as no surprise to Mrs. Miller. She'd known about Michael's lifestyle for some time now. She'd hoped it was just a phase or that he would come to his senses and straighten up. As time went by, she gave up on these hopes and gave into the fact that she was going to have to do something. She'd been dreading a night like this and had talked herself blue in the face pleading with Michael to be careful. She could see his face as she explained how dangerous drinking and drugging could be. She remembered how he rolled his eyes as she told him about how his grandfather had drunk himself to death. Michael claimed to be different, indestructible, and even bullet-proof. Nothing she said could reach him. Michael felt different, special, and maybe even a bit immortal. Others got hurt; but not him. He'd be okay. He told her to back off and quit being such a nag. He told her he wasn't his grandfather and that he knew how to drink responsibly. He told her that he wouldn't let anything bad happen to him. And, he was sort of right; that night he was okay, but his best friend wasn't.

Seeing his buddy's mangled corpse on the paramedic stretcher changed things. In its most brutal form, truth propelled him and slammed him down with eye-opening results. Eye-opening and gut-wrenching perceptions poured in. He saw the horror and heartbreak on Brian's parents face that night as they rushed into the emergency room. He saw Brian's mom fall to the floor as the doctor informed her that there was nothing that could be done. He saw anguish on the dad's face that would haunt him for many years.

As he sat in the waiting room of that hospital, Michael vaguely recalled something his mother had shared awhile back. He remembered how she described descending into the hell of her childhood after her dad died. How she would lie awake at night praying to hear his car pull up to the house. She told Michael about how her own mother worried herself sick and almost died of heartbreak after dad died. She recalled how her father had gone out one night and in one slow motion heart shattering moment never came home. He went out for a ride and never came back.

Mom talked about how much her own mother had been wounded by his death, and how empty the house was without dad's loud boisterous laugh. She told him that no one ever laughed in that house again and that she couldn't wait to get out and step back into the sunshine. Mom explained how she met the most wonderful man in the world, married him and had a beautiful baby boy named Michael. Michael recalled his mother's eyes as she shared with him the excitement she felt about her own family and how different things would be for them. Michael heard how in his family tree, alcohol had served as a solvent; it removed paint from wood, dirt from glass, linings from stomachs, fathers from children, husbands from wives and friends from life.

Michael sat in that emergency room and felt a sense of overbearing sadness, not just for his friend's parents, but for his mother and all she'd lived through. He cringed and alternated between racking sobs and wrenching guilt. He cried for his friend and for his mother. In his own way he was crushed that night, not by a rolling car, but by an overwhelming sense of guilt for contributing to his mom's misery. What was wrong with him? Why in the world did he put her through such pain? He had plenty of reasons to change, but just simply wouldn't or maybe he couldn't.

It was as if there were two Michaels—the inside Michael, who was sensitive and loving, and the outside Michael, who was dishonest, manipulative, deceitful and angry. He was bombarded by a foreboding sense that he was just like his father and grandfather. He wasn't going to be the person he'd always thought he could be. Alcohol had become his friend and enemy at the same time. Living with it was too painful; living without it was worse. Michael's use caused emotional pain and his emotional pain contributed toward his use. A vicious cycle needed interrupting.

This interruption came as horribly disguised gift from Brian. One week after his friend's funeral, Michael sat in his bedroom and at 2:00 AM, took what he thought was a lethal dose of sleeping pills from mom's medicine cabinet. He woke up the next day in a psychiatric hospital. The spectacle of the grim reaper's visit had not only taken his best friend away, but had removed Michael's delusions. His world began to implode on him. While in the hospital, mom agreed to schedule a chemical dependency assessment for Michael. He subsequently entered a residential chemical dependency treatment center for adolescents to treat the same disease that had killed his best friend, stolen his father, removed his grandfather and smashed his mother's spirit.

Though treatment was by no means a picnic, Michael found that once again he was able to make a promise and keep it. He learned that alcoholism is a disease and not the result of some moral weakness. He wasn't stupid or bad; he didn't make himself an addict and couldn't unmake himself one either. He learned about his genetic predisposition and how genetics loaded the gun and his environment pulled the trigger. Michael began a process of self-discovery and self-forgiveness. He and his mom spent hours in counseling, healing the cuts and bruises his illness had caused. After six weeks of hard work and gut wrenching honesty, Michael was discharged from treatment with a commitment to get a sponsor and attend at least five A.A. meetings a week.

Recovery didn't just teach him how to stay sober, but how also to enjoy life without chemicals. Michael's descent into the disease scarred him, but the ascent strengthened him. Once a month, Michael visits the grave of his best friend who was killed that awful night so long ago. It was one year ago that Michael's friend lost his life and one year ago that Michael began to gain his life back. There are times when Michael still feels it should have been him that died. Michael's mom has once again begun to laugh and Michael has begun to make sense out of his friend's death. In dying, maybe his friend gave Michael the best gift of all, a sober life.

*I am only one,*
*but still I am one.*
*I cannot do everything,*
*But still I can do something;*
*And because I cannot do everything*
*I will not refuse to do the something that I can do.*
—*Edward Everett Hale*

## Classroom Interventions: One Size Doesn't Fit All

This section will focus on the intervention process. An essential aspect of intervening is the use of consequences. Adults intervene with kids in several ways: *redirection, natural consequences, imposed consequences, restoration and time out.*

1. **Redirection**—Redirection is when a particular behavior is interrupted or stopped before it gets worse. Adults have been redirecting kids for as long as there have been kids. Because redirection is preventative, this section includes a significant amount of pertinent information. When redirection is effective, the following are not needed near as much.
2. **Natural consequences**—This is allowing consequences to occur that are a direct result of a specific behavior or decision made by a student.
3. **Imposed consequences**—This is when the adult structures or imposes a consequence for a specific behavior or decision.
4. **Restoration**—Restoration is when the student is expected to fix or clean up the mess or damage he or she has done.
5. **Time out**—Temporarily removing a child from a situation as a result of his or her behavior or decisions.

## It is There Even When Unseen

When we consider the very wide array of problems, tragedies, traumas, accidents, mistakes and transgressions that occur in families, we recognize that there really are no level playing fields. Divorce, alcoholism, violence, mental illness, abuse, neglect, extreme poverty, abandonment, ridicule and bullying occur outside of school, only to be brought to the classroom on a daily basis. Because of learned responses, lack of experience, immaturity or "wiring", a student may behave very inappropriately and not be aware of it.

Unresolved and often misdirected anger, internalized fear, strong feelings of inadequacy and insignificance can be right under the surface of students' behaviors in the classroom. The inability to know how to deal with these kinds of feelings often results in some form of acting out or withdrawal. Evidence suggests this inability is tied to developmental stages and age. As we get older, we usually gain knowledge, experience and wisdom about how to express feelings.

So, considering all things known and unknown about a particular child, what he or she is doing probably makes sense. Not that it is acceptable or tolerated, but it at least makes sense. If we were privy to all of the fires and explosions in a young girl's head, we might immediately exclaim, "no wonder she acts this way!"

## Possible Reasons Children Misbehave

Grief
For attention
Scapegoat role
Testing teacher's boundaries
Post Traumatic Stress Disorder
Feel ill, bored, hungry or sleepy
Asserting sense of empowerment
Lack of accurate information and prior experience
Previously "rewarded" for their misbehavior with adult attention

## Making it Effective

An intervention is a method where leverage is applied to encourage positive change. That leverage varies depending on the situation and the individuals involved. For example, an administrator may encourage a student to get help by offering two options—assistance or suspension. The student and parent make the choice, but the administrator makes one choice more appealing than the other. Judges and probation officers have been doing this type of intervention for years (at least some have).

Although it may seem obvious, when we intervene, we need to determine what it is we are attempting to accomplish. In the broadest sense, an intervention is any effort that is designed to bring about positive changes in another person's behavior. Unfortunately, if we leave the definition that broad, some will assume that pleading, begging, threatening, or bribing are effective intervention techniques, which they are not.

Interventions don't just happen in the principal's office. They occur in the classroom, hallway, cafeteria, gymnasium, counselor's office, and practice field. In this section, we will examine the intervention process as it may occur in several settings. But first, we must take a look at those things that are essential to an effective intervention, regardless of the setting.

*"Considering all things about a student's life, what is known and unknown, the behavior we see may very well make sense."*
### Anna Allen

Anna's quote does not suggest that the behavior be tolerated; this would be blatantly foolish and definitely considered enabling. It is important to recognize that what the student is doing is for some reason; nothing happens by accident. This does not excuse the behavior, but it does help us not to personalize the situation. We all need the reminder that a person and his or her behavior are not the same thing; they need to be seen as separate. Behavior can be very bad, while a person is basically very good. Successful interventions deal with the behavior while supporting the person. It may seem a paradox, but this premise is essential to conducting successful interventions.

# Essential Points to Remember about Intervening

☞ The purpose of intervention is to interrupt the behavior and motivate the student to make positive changes.

☞ The intervention focuses on behavior while treating the person with dignity.

☞ The more specific and objective the words, the more effective the intervention.

☞ Avoid attempting to guess why the student is acting out or distressed.

☞ Remain detached, becoming angry or judgmental will prevent success.

☞ Remain on track and avoid prolonged tangents.

☞ Avoid words that are inflammatory. Substitute *concern* for *problem*.

☞ Do not personalize the student's reaction; it isn't about you.

☞ Do not attempt to intervene around peers; remove the student so the conversation is private.

☞ Have a clear idea of what you want from the students and communicate it directly.

☞ Do not assume students automatically know the alternatives to negative behavior.

To effectively intervene, we need to focus on specific behaviors and describe them in such a way that the student or parent can hear it. Generalizations and interpretations are discouraged; they tend to result in defensiveness. Blanket statements regarding the behaviors tend to leave gaps for argument and debate—perfect ingredients for a power struggle. The following two statements are attempts to address the same behavior—tardiness. The first is general and the other is specific.

**Generalized statement**
*"You're always late for class."*

**Specific statement**
*"On Monday, Tuesday, and Friday of this week you were ten minutes late to my class."*

Even if the student has been tardy 99 out of 100 times, generalized statements, such as the first one above, leave us open to being inaccurate, when instead we can make statements that are accurate and non-debatable.

*"Listen or thy tongue will keep thee deaf."*
**Native American Proverb**

# Chapter 14

# Ears Do Not Always Hear

## Using Words, Tone of Voice, Expression and Posture

An effective school intervention is not considered to be formal therapy or treatment. It is an attempt to decrease the agitation or distress interfering with learning. In almost every case, the success of a school intervention is based on dialogue or a verbal transaction. Most communication is nonverbal: *eye contact, facial expression, posture, gesture, and tone of voice.* This accounts for about 80%-90% of normal communication. Clearly, the verbal component is important. Paraphrasing lets the student know he or she is being heard. Sounds such as, *"uh hum", "go on", "um",* encourage the speaker. Certainly words are important and when poorly chosen can sabotage an attempt to reach a student. Based on the responses, the student should be able to tell the other person is listening.

We know that hearing and listening are not the same thing. One can have perfect hearing and not listen worth a hoot. People who are hearing impaired and cannot hear a thing can be good listeners. *Active listening* is a learned skill that demonstrates to the speaker that someone is paying attention and interested in what is being said. Any type of intervention requires *active listening.* People need to vent or discharge some energy during or after a conflict. Venting allows the person to settle down. Being able to talk about the incident is healing. Not being told that feelings are wrong is also a big factor in active listening.

## Do you . . . ?

Make eye contact?
Appear interested in the speaker?
Encourage the speaker with words or sounds?
Use paraphrasing and summarizing?
Ask the right kind of questions?
Use a tone or voice that indicates interest?
Remain on track and avoid interruption?
Let the speaker do more talking than you?
Respect the physical space around the listener?
Remember what the speaker says?

## Verbal Skills Used in Listening

**Encouragers**—Words or sounds that encourage the speaker to continue such as *"uh, hum!"* and *"go on!"*

**Summarizing**—Using different words, in a shorter time, capturing the jest of what has been said.

**Paraphrasing**—Restating back to the speaker what has been said, using your own words.

**Volume, Tone and Inflection**—These account for a great deal in positive communication, even more than words alone.

## Open and Closed-Ended Questions

Part of an intervention process may call for getting information from the student or parent. How questions are posed have a great deal to do with how much information you get.

### Open-ended

Asked in a way that it takes a sentence or more to answer. You get more information and the student gets to vent.

Sample: *"What is it about my class that disappoints you?"*

### Closed—ended

Asked in such a way that the answer is "yes" or "no". When time is short or the student/parent is long-winded, closed-ended questions can bring the conversation to an end.

Sample: *"Don't you like my class?"*

### Body Posture

Most of these postures use common sense and you just need to be aware of how you are sitting. Sitting slouched; acting fidgety or laconic can shut down the interaction in a second. Sitting up or forward displays interest. Hand gestures can emphasize an important point. Arms crossed too tightly suggest being closed off from the speaker. Yet, there is nothing wrong with folding your arms. It is the "too tightly" approach that separates one from the other.

### Expressions & Eye Contact

Facial expressions can say more in an instance, than speaking twenty words in a minute. Some of us are more expressive while others tend to be more restricted. Usually raised eyebrows show interest or the need to ask a question. A wrinkled forehead can show anger, disagreement or puzzlement.

Eye contact makes it all personal and sometimes intimate. Similar to crossed arms, it is okay to not always stare at the speaker. Looking away is a natural tendency. It is when no eye contact is made that communication is hampered. We have all spoken with a person who refused to look us in the eye. You can move to the left or right, trying to get some eye contact, and the person will shift in order to avoid it.

## You Probably Shouldn't . . .

The following phrases or actions interrupt effective listening.

Take the person's inventory—acting as if you are some type of judge.
Step on the other person's sentences before he or she is through.
Sit with a desk between you and the speaker.
Speak harshly.
Allow your thoughts to drift or daydream.
Say "me too".
Interrupt the speaker.
Change the subject without reason.
Give advice when not asked for.
Sound condescending.
Act shocked by what the speaker says.
Expect openness if not in a confidential setting.
Act like you heard something when you did not; check it out.
Take a phone call or text message while listening.
Dominate the conversation.

*"Those who know how to win are much more numerous than those who know how to make proper use of their victories."*
**Polybius"**

## A Solution-Focused Approach
*What If Both Could Win?*

Interactions between adults and disruptive or acting out students tend to lean towards the "I win and you lose" style of communicating, where the adult displays power and the student submits (or is supposed to). Some kids do not submit very easily and would rather go "down in flames" than appear to give in. Power struggles leave someone defeated, usually the student. Interactions that are based on a win-win outcome meet the needs of both. The hierarchy is maintained for the adult and the student is appropriately empowered (which goes a long way towards resolution). Below are some examples of interactions between a teacher and a student. The interaction may be more a reaction than actually communication

### Scenario 1
A student in class constantly gets out of his chair, disrupting others. He refuses to participate and often appears to be sleeping.

### The Reactive Teacher

*"I told you at least a hundred times to go back to your chair. Do you want to be sent to the office?"*

The response is predictable. A power struggle has ensued; the student is backed into an ego-driven emotional corner. To resolve, the adult wins and the student loses! Taking the exact same situation, the entire interaction can be much more pleasant and effective. *Validation, acceptance and respect* are the vital ingredients to employ when working with traumatized kids. The conversation might look something like this:

## Reframed Response

*"I noticed you're having a difficult time staying in your chair today as well as being part of this class. You seem a bit agitated, maybe even upset about something. Is there anything I can help you with?"*

This method works to prevent an immediate and automatic defensive posture by the student. An "I win and you win" approach is beneficial even if the student refuses to interact. If he does not respond well to this style, it is doubtful the student will respond well to being challenged and threatened. At the very least, the rest of the class observes a student being treated with respect and dignity, rather than power and control.

*Reframing* is taking a troubled situation and shifting it from the "what is wrong" mindset to a "what was done right" perspective. This does not let the student off the hook; kids do need to be accountable for their actions. It does promote solutions rather than failures. Below are several examples of statements from two teachers contrasting these two very different styles:

### Scenario 2
A student who has a pattern of being tardy just walked into class late.

### Reactive
*"Why are you always late for class? Everyone else gets here on time! What's your problem?"*

### Reframed
*"On the days when you come to class on time, what are the things you do to help get you here? I know you figured out a way to be on time. I've seen you do it."*

### Scenario 3
Frustrated, a student threatens to walk out and quit school saying, *"I'm through with this place; tomorrow I'll quit school and get my G.E.D. This class blows!"*

### Reactive

*"You might just as well quit with that attitude! I'd say it is your attitude that's a problem around here, not school or this class! It really doesn't matter since the others around here are sick of your negative attitude."*

### Reframed

*"I can see you are frustrated. You were talking about graduating a few weeks ago; what changed? There was a time you seemed to enjoy coming to my class. What do you think made it okay then?"*

### Scenario 4

A student makes a physical threat about another student who betrayed her confidence saying, *"I'm sick and tired of her running her big mouth! I'll shut it for her since she can't do it herself. I'm going to get her after class".*

### Reactive

*"If you say something like that again, young lady, I'll not only send you to the office, I'll call your mother at work. Is this what you want? Huh?"*

### Reframed

*"It sounds like you are really feeling betrayed right now and are struggling with how to best respond. Other than fighting, what are some of the alternatives that can make things better?"*

*Reframing* may appear to be too "touchy-feely" or syrupy for some, but it works. It takes no more time to reframe a statement than it takes to control and dominate. Reframing is not a magic bullet and some students need much more intervention than this kind of interaction. When attempts have failed to redirect or interrupt a student's behavior or attitude, a referral (*identification*) to the student assistance program (SAP) or other intervention team may be appropriate. The student may be displaying similar behaviors in her other classes as well. The SAP or other intervention team is able to gather what is happening in all classes and see the big picture. Once a screening is completed, then appropriate interventions are implemented.

*"There is nothing more galling to angry people than the coolness of those on whom they wish to vent their spleen."*
**Alexandre Dumas**

## Expecting Anger and Resistance

Whether resulting from frustration, disappointment, violation, unfairness, trauma or just a bad hair day, some degree of anger simmers in most people. At times this simmering boils to the point of scalding those around. Though a real feeling, anger is secondary. Other feelings come first and convert to anger and/or rage. For example, if a friend betrays a secret you entrusted and rumors spread, you would most likely feel anger. Anger is normal and an expected human reaction, but preceding it are feelings such as *hurt, betrayal, humiliation, violation, and sadness*. Anger is an effective way to avoid more sensitive feelings. It deflects those too painful to discuss, or even think about. When angry, kids often need to vent appropriately. There are healthy ways of venting that do not have to be hurtful or out of line. It is best to interact with the student away from peers to minimize the tendency for him to perform. Pride and ego are right around the corner, just waiting to step in and inflate. When communicating, it is essential to use active listening skills and it helps to have a connection with the student; trust is essential for a student to even attempt to express feelings.

Being angry doesn't give permission for a student to be rude, aggressive or combative with others. There is a difference between expressing feelings and acting on them. No one should tolerate being abused, physically or verbally. Everyone's boundaries need to be honored and respected. If a student steps over the line with aggression, appropriate action needs to be taken, regardless of the trauma. Having a reason for the feelings is not an excuse for the behavior. There will be situations that no amount of skilled intervening helps. There are limitations to everything at some point in time.

*"A failure is a man who has blundered but is not capable of cashing in on the experience."*
**Elbert Hubbard**

# Chapter 15

# Working with One Student

There are few adults who intentionally hurt kids. There are quite a few who do it unintentionally. The best and most effective teachers will at some point say or do something that is hurtful and reactive. Progress is more realistic than perfection. When progress is isolated by one incident, the previous statement probably doesn't do much harm. If the "once in a while" becomes a pattern or habit, something should be altered before damage is done. A teacher can have a huge impact on self-esteem that will last a long time.

## It Isn't About You

Contrary to how it feels, the student's behavior isn't always about the teacher. Taking it personally only takes away your ability to remain objective. Statements and decisions are made based on strong feelings, which we often have to retract. Not only is it not about you, it might not even be about the student. Remember, there is a reason for everything; nothing is "just because." We just do not have knowledge of the many variables and factors that explain what we are seeing.

Last night, Sherry heard her little sister cry herself to sleep again! Mom and dad had another bad fight. Names were spoken with vicious voices; words were used that were profane. Threats were made that were at one time unthinkable. She remembers the last words she heard as she crouched in bed trying to shut her ears, "I'm taking these kids out of here and you'll never see them again!" This is followed by a desperate plea, begging for a truce. But it doesn't help. Dad rages when he's mad. Dad says mean things when he's like this. Dad does hurtful things when he's angry. And, last night he was the angriest Sherry had ever witnessed.

*"Who cares what you think; you're not my mother!"* You have no idea what is going on in her personal life. All you know is she just took a defiant and offensive stand with you in front of the class. Immediately you feel the heat under your collar. You feel the quickened jump in your pulse. In what seems like an instant reaction, you challenge her with an, *"I dare you to speak that way to me, young lady. Let's see what your parents think about your rude mouth!"* This response triggers more self-defeating comments by Sherry until it escalates into a full blown referral, parent conference, in-school suspension or placement at an alternative campus.

The question is, would you respond the same way knowing about Sherry's fear and pain? Could you have addressed the rudeness while supporting Sherry? You know, "hate the sin, not the sinner?" In the actual moment of the interchange, things can go in two very different directions. Either she shuts down more, gets in trouble and builds more resentment, or she feels respected and supported and acts very contrite about her outburst.

In looking at what is potentially harmful, there are things so self-evident that it is a wonder they are done at all. They may be blatantly obvious, but they are done never the less. Some of these include:

## Techniques That Simply Do Not Work

Shaming, insulting, bullying and humiliating
Seeking revenge, using sarcasm, invalidating or being cruel
Blaming, discouraging, criticizing and ganging up
Screaming, embarrassing, hitting, isolating and
Saying: "You are stupid, you are bad, or you are worthless."

## A Good Idea

See the behavior and the person as separate.
Treat others as you would have them treat you.

Continually stating to a child phrases such as, *"Stop that!" "Don't do it that way!"* or *"You never . . ."* is harmful to a child's self-esteem. Discipline techniques such as removal from the group, or isolation in a time-out chair or a corner may have negative consequences for the child.

There needs to be a reality check at this point in order to consider that there are so many different situations that arise in class, the cafeteria, the hallway, and the gym, etc. Sometimes the most competent adult who works with children will overstep the line and engage in a form of discipline that may be regretted later. Remember that distress patterns occur and can be re-stimulated by a student's words, attitude or actions.

Under normal circumstances, we are able to stay on top of what we say and how we react. Our intellect is in control and keeps our emotions from taking the lead. Emotions are important but not what should drive our behavior or comments. When buttons are pushed, there is a flip-flop, our emotions take charge, and we say and do things we later regret. Our intellect takes a backseat in how we interact with students.

*We will make mistakes; it is part of being human. The goal is to minimize the frequency or extent in which the mistakes occur.*

## Approaches to Discipline Really Should

Increase initiative
Promote self-esteem
Encourage cooperation
Give a sense of being valued
Teach responsibility for what happens
Motivate taking responsibility rather than blaming others
Help students relate successfully to others, and solve problems

## Reframing Revisited

As discussed earlier, reframing is restating a situation in such a way that it recognizes efforts and acknowledges the positive side of situations. In almost every situation there is some positive aspect that can be emphasized. This is not some naïve approach from the *"Brady Bunch"*. This positive approach allows the conversation to be redirected with less resistance. With some familiarity, reframing becomes a comfortable and effective way to engage with students.

### Scenario 5

The following examples are statements made to a student who consistently interrupts you when you speak.

### Reacting

*"Why do you always interrupt me? You're rude; just keep it up. You hear?"*

### Reframing

*"When you start talking when I am speaking, it makes it hard for me to get my point across. I don't think that is what you are trying to do. Tell me about the last time when you really wanted to say something, yet managed to wait until it was time!"*

Both of these statements intend to keep the student quiet, but one is much more positive than the other is. It isn't too hard to decide which of these statements would get the best response. Taking the positive tack does not excuse the behavior, but does encourage the student to explore why the behavior occurred in the first place.

### Scenario 6
Another example that is more challenging might be a student who cusses out another student while in class. It might look like this:

### Reacting
*"Are you kidding? You think you can talk like a trash-mouth in my class and get away with it, buddy? I'll have you know that no one, I repeat no one cusses in my class. You will stay after school to just think about your language."*

### Reframing
*"Whoa! That was a mean thing to say. Obvious you are angry and are having some trouble expressing yourself. It happens to a lot of people at some point. My concern is that it not only is mean, it affects our whole classroom. I bet you've been angry before and managed to not cuss; why were you successful then? Also, I think you understand that I can't let those words be said without some consequences. Would you rather stay after school or go to see the principal?"*

## Too Touchy Feely?

You might be saying right now; *"Sure, it sounds good on paper when you have the time to think about the response. But come on, be realistic."*

It is not time that is a problem; reframing may take less than a minute. It deals with the situation, includes consequences, teaches responsibility, promotes introspection and has an impact on the overall class.

The resistance is about doing things differently. Change is difficult and always meets skepticism. And, there are adults who simply don't want to treat kids this way. It seems they prefer reacting, where the student is embarrassed, insulted, and treated as if stupid. It isn't saving time that drives this behavior; it is choosing to be hurtful . . . Enough said.

## Reasons Interventions May Not Work

Feelings negated
Statements were not specific
Judgmental attitude
Failure to develop an alliance
Enabling
Lack of clarity
Condescending attitude towards student and/or parents
Making assumptions
Intervention attempted in front of an audience

*"The first step binds one to the second."*
**French Proverb**

## Redirecting Distress Patterns

### Interrupting the Behavior

Without a doubt, it is the relationship that promotes successful redirection, not the technique. Regardless of the merit of the steps listed below, unless there is some relationship between the adult and student, these steps probably will not work well. When a student's distress pattern is interfering with class or teaching, the following suggestions have been known to help. These steps need to remain flexible and be adjusted to the needs of the student.

1. Temporarily remove student from peers. Attempting to re-direct in front of peers tends to feed the need for the student to "save face" and perform for others. By removing the student in a way that allows the student's dignity to stay intact, the opportunity for success is increased. This is a good way of starting on the right foot!

2. Maintain positive regard for the student, but not the behavior (perceive the behavior and the student as separate). Avoid acting angry, and instead remain calm and matter-of-fact. If the student perceives that he or she is not liked (judged), then redirecting most likely won't work. At the same time, you are not asked to act any more positive than is realistic. Being matter-of-fact is a good approach. This not a request that you be cheerful; you just need to not be visibly angry. You can have all the feelings you want; just don't act on them.

3. Avoid being re-stimulated yourself. Students know how to push buttons and get responses. Detachment and objectivity are two things that need to be achieved or maintained. You must remain emotionally detached and not react to the student's behavior. There are times when this is very difficult and when so, it is important to be aware. If your buttons do get pushed, you might postpone the conversation until you are in a better place emotionally.

4. Validate the efforts made by the student. Remember, considering all things known and unknown, what the student is doing probably makes sense, even though it is not acceptable. In a case where the student is

resisting participating in class, the validation could be that considering how he or she feels, you are impressed that the student came to class at all. This does not mean the resistance is not addressed. Validation is acknowledging the effort put forth by the student, even when it falls short of expectations. This step makes the student more accepting of what is said next.

5. Specifically identify the concerns presented. Help the student understand that the resistance may be the result of being temporarily overwhelmed, but that it is interfering with participation. Help the student to see that his or her attitude, in fact, may be working against his or her own best interests. This is where you try to get the student to understand the concept of "shooting oneself in the foot."

6. State specific expectations about what is expected in class and ask the student for some suggestions that you can use to help to remind him or her of these expectations. When the student is re-stimulated at a later time (and it will happen), the suggestion can help to interrupt the distress pattern. By having the student contribute suggestions, it implies that his or her ownership is important and that you understand making changes is often difficult.

7. Reaffirm the mutual alliance between the student and yourself that each and every time the pattern (behavior or attitude) arises in class, it will be addressed. Ask the student for that same commitment and acknowledge that it may be hard for the student to make the needed changes, but not impossible.

8. If repeated attempts do not result in redirected behavior, it may be indicative of something more serious going on and you should consider a referral to an early intervention team or the Student Assistance Program.

*"Mr. President, do you wear boxers or briefs?"*
**College Student to President Bill Clinton**

## Boundaries and Self-Disclosure

Students will ask questions that may be innocent, but are a violation of a teacher's boundaries. Determining how much personal information to share with students is up to each one of us. Caution must be considered when one is reminded of what kids often do with information such as answers to the following questions:

### A Student Oversteps the Boundaries
*"Did you have sex before marriage?"*
*"How much money do you make?"*
*"Did you do drugs in high school?"*

### Example Responses from the Teacher
*"I find that question inappropriate."*
*"There are some things that are not your business."*
*"Why is what I did or didn't do important to you?"*
*"I will not answer that question; don't ask it again."*
*"This class is about you and your education; it isn't about me."*

It is okay to feel angry with a student because he or she crosses your boundaries. Model a healthy expression of your feelings, rather than pretend the feelings do not exist.

There are situations when some self-disclosure is appropriate. If sharing information with a student contributes to the goal or purpose of the conversation, it may be something to consider. Sometimes the line between good disclosure and a mistake is thin and blurry. If in doubt, it is best not to share personal information.

Answering a question like, "Did you have trouble with homework when you were in school?", can strengthen the connection between a teacher and student. Showing a student a degree of fallibility promotes trust and respect. Kids see through an adult's pretence that he or she is beyond mistakes. There are teachers who choose to be real with students, rather than constantly on guard and defensive. Students tend to like this about a teacher. There is a paradox where showing fallibility strengthens respect. Admitting mistakes promotes trust.

*"Where does discipline end? Where does punishment begin? Somewhere between these, thousands of children inhabit a voiceless hell."*
**Francois Murcia**

# Chapter 16

# Working with Many

### Managing the Classroom

Most teachers receive little formal instruction when it comes to classroom management. In the four or more years of pursuing a teaching degree, how many hours were devoted to such an important skill set? Without a road map of some sort, people are left to their own devices on how to discipline. Falling back on the only experience one has often results in a teacher replicating discipline learned from childhood. If shame and humiliation were the primary way a child received discipline, then when grown, it is no real surprise to see the same techniques used in the classroom.

Discipline and punishment are not interchangeable words. Discipline is when the student knows ahead of time what the consequences will be for a specific behavior. Punishment is when the child is unaware of stepping over the line, yet is given consequences as if already warned. To discipline is to teach, redirect and help. Punishment is a way to make someone suffer for his or her actions without offering rehabilitation, treatment, training or teaching.

*Feelings are real and legitimate; children behave and misbehave for a reason,
even if adults cannot understand.*
*"Management works in the system; Leadership works on the system."*
**Stephen Covey**

## Classroom Management

Just as it is in any family, the classroom is an entity unto itself. Though made up of many individuals, they all come together to form a single entity, the classroom. Using systemic dynamics, this entity has its own spoken and unspoken rules and contains the same survival roles we see in families. There is a hierarchy of influence and a need for structure and consistency. Just like in the family, a classroom can be healthy or dysfunctional; it primarily depends on the teacher. Hierarchy in class is seen as the evidence of control by a teacher. More accurately, it represents an environment where students can count on a teacher to keep things safe, secure and exciting. As valuable as hierarchy is, it shouldn't be confused with excessive-control, rigidity, or blind obedience to rules. Hierarchy is ensuring that students know who is in charge. It is the student being aware that final decisions and the direction of class are up to the teacher. Hierarchy can be defined as the ability to allow kids some freedom, with full knowledge that this freedom is given, not taken. There is always a reason for a particular action or behavior. This is not the same thing as an excuse. "Reason" implies that outside factors do contribute, yet people are still accountable. "Excuse" implies that the person cannot help him or herself and is not accountable for behavior.

## Promoting Classroom Management

Howard Miller, Associate Professor of Education at Lincoln University (Jefferson City, Missouri), suggests 12 steps teachers can take at the beginning of the year to promote effective classroom management.

1. Develop a set of written expectations you can enforce.
2. Be consistent. Be consistent. Be consistent.
3. Be patient with yourself and with your students.
4. Make parents your allies. Call early and often.

5.  Don't talk too much. Use the first 15 minutes of class for lectures or presentations, then get the kids working.
6.  Break the class period into two or three different activities.
7.  Begin at the very beginning of each class period and end at the very end.
8.  Don't roll call. Take the roll with your seating chart while students are working.
9.  Keep all students actively involved.
10. Discipline individual students quietly and privately.
11. Keep your sense of perspective and your sense of humor.
12. Know when to ask for help.

The more effective the classroom management, the fewer incidents of acting out there will be. The classroom is a system and all systems take on a life of their own, some healthy, some dysfunctional. The healthier the classroom, the better the learning.

## Different Personality, Different Style

We all have a way of doing things that feels quite natural and is our "default" position when reacting to a situation. The four primary styles are listed below. What is your style?

## Authoritarian

**The authoritarian teacher places firm limits and controls on the students.**

√   Students will often have assigned seats for the entire term.
√   The desks are usually in straight rows and there are no deviations.
√   Students must be in their seats at the beginning of class and they frequently remain there throughout the period.
√   This teacher rarely gives hall passes or recognizes excused absences.
√   Often, the classroom is quiet. Students know they should not interrupt the teacher.

√ Since verbal exchange and discussion are discouraged, the authoritarian's students do not have the opportunity to learn and/or practice communication skills.

√ This teacher prefers vigorous discipline and expects swift obedience.

√ Failure to obey the teacher usually results in detention or a trip to the principal's office.

√ In this classroom, students need to follow directions and not ask why.

√ At the extreme, the authoritarian teacher gives no indication that he\she cares for the students.

√ Students in this class are likely to be reluctant to initiate activity, since they may feel powerless.

## Laissez-faire

**The laissez-faire teacher places few demands or controls on the students.**

√ "Do your own thing" describes this classroom.

√ This teacher accepts the students' impulses and actions and is less likely to monitor their behavior.

√ This overindulgent style is associated with students' lack of social competence and self-control.

√ It is difficult for students to learn socially acceptable behavior when the teacher is so permissive.

√ With few demands placed upon them, these students frequently have a lower motivation to achieve.

## Authoritative

**The authoritative teacher places limits and controls on the students, but simultaneously encourages independence.**

√ This teacher often explains the reasons behind the rules and decisions.

√ If a student is disruptive, the teacher offers a polite, but firm, reprimand.

√ This teacher sometimes disciplines, but only after careful consideration of the circumstances.

√   The authoritative teacher is also open to considerable verbal interaction, including critical debates.

√   The students know that they can interrupt the teacher, if they have a relevant question or comment.

√   This environment offers the students the opportunity to learn and practice communication skills.

## Indifferent

**The indifferent teacher is not very involved in the classroom.**

√   This teacher places few demands, if any, on the students and appears generally disinterested.

√   The indifferent teacher just doesn't want to impose on the students.

√   As such, he/she often feels that class preparation is not worth the effort.

√   Things like field trips and special projects are out of the question.

√   This teacher simply won't allow for the necessary preparation time.

√   Sometimes, he/she will use the same materials, year after year.

√   Also, classroom discipline is lacking.

√   This teacher may lack the skills, confidence, or courage to discipline students.

√   The students sense and reflect the teacher's indifferent attitude. Accordingly, very little learning occurs. Everyone is just "going through the motions" and killing time.

√   In this aloof environment, the students have very few opportunities to observe or practice communication skills.

√   With few demands placed on them and very little discipline, students have low achievement motivation and lack self-control.

## A Better Way?

On the following page are three samples of how a teacher manages his or her classroom. The styles range from rigid control to letting anarchy rule. Fortunately, one of the styles represents an excellent balance of control and flexibility on the teacher's part. Like water in your palm, it is best held when your hands are unclenched. Squeeze too much and it all leaks out. Rigid control might result in little acting out, but it also results in less learning. Spontaneity and appropriate risk-taking seem to be essential components to healthy learning.

Take a look at how Mr. Anderson, Ms. Perez and Ms. Cook facilitate their respective classrooms to see how different each is.

1.  Mr. Anderson is known for the absolute control he exercises over his sophomore English class. An observer would witness students sitting orderly at their desks, with no side talk. Questions are asked only after being called upon, which requires a hand raised high. The observer might see less laughter than is seen in other classes, even other English classes. Mr. Anderson is an excellent guard and prides himself on not letting the students get by with anything. The pall that hangs over the classroom prevents spontaneity, enthusiasm, curiosity, awe and satisfaction from finding a home.

2.  Next door, Ms. Perez teaches ninth grade English. Anyone walking by the class might see students working in small groups, several conversations going on at the same time and the teacher casually moving about the classroom. The teacher is encouraging students and sometimes the class might appear to be disorganized. Yet, upon further observation, it becomes clear that learning is fun in this class. It is also apparent that the students like and respect Ms. Perez and she likes them.

3.  Across the hall, Ms. Cook teaches tenth grade English. Walking by this class is frustrating, because every time the classroom is in chaos. The noise and lack of control are such that the students can't hear Ms. Cook's voice. Even if they could, students in this class would ignore it. Kids are seen gathering in small groups to discuss what happened last night at a party, or to discuss who is messing around with someone's boyfriend. Scattered throughout this class is a handful of students who are sitting, trying to read an assignment and shaking their heads in sad disappointment that every day is like this. Curriculum is lost, learning is diminished and anarchy rules. By the way, many of the same students are in other classes and don't act out with such abandonment.

*"There is so much good in the worst of us, and so much bad in the best of us,*
*That it hardly becomes any of us, to talk about the rest of us."*
**Anonymous (c. 1900)**

We have three very different styles of classroom management in this particular hallway. There is Mr. Anderson, the tight fisted, and chest puffed up, drill sergeant. Across the hall there is Ms. Cook, the hands off, liaise fare approach (or lack of approach). In the class of Ms. Perez, we see an environment that appears relaxed, focused and on task.

In defense of Mr. Anderson and Ms. Cook, the teachers in this school have been left on their own to exercise a style of classroom management. They are generally unaware of different ways to discipline students and rely upon what "they've figured out on their own!" Sometimes, the teachers end up replicating similar parenting styles their parents may have used. These parenting practices may include shaming, ridicule, threats, laser-eyed looks, and condescending expressions. Getting a teaching degree doesn't necessarily mean that one possesses expertise in dealing with acting out behaviors, or effective classroom management.

Students require a learning environment that is able to balance a form of classroom management that supports self-esteem and at the same time has enough discipline to avoid anarchy. How this balance is achieved often varies, based on personalities. Your style is uniquely yours; it isn't a choice so much as an "instinct". It is learned, but in a way that we are unaware of the ongoing lessons.

## Remember . . .

Do not lose sight of the fact that it is the relationship you have with your students that empowers you to be effective when intervening. A student will listen and respond to someone he or she likes much more than someone who is disliked and mistrusted. Do not confuse consistency for rigidity, nor firmness for mean-spirited. Empowering a student is not giving up your hierarchical standing; it is getting the student to take ownership in being part of the solution.

## Exacerbate or De-escalate?

### Scenario 7

In class, Robert continues to talk and when told to knock it off, he gets angry. His anger is evident through his tone of voice, the volume and his words. Though not profane, his words are inappropriate and are not tolerated by his teacher. She says . . .

### Teacher

*"What did I just hear you say? Oh, tell me you didn't call me stupid? Say it again so I can see you say it this time. As a matter of fact, the entire class is waiting to hear just how stupid you can be. Say it again if you're brave enough to say it to my face."*

Put yourself in Robert's place and speculate your own response. Challenged in front of the class, he needs to save face. Another way of responding to the exact same situation might sound like this:

### Teacher

*"Robert, you sound angry today. What's going on? You normally don't talk to me that way. Can we step out in the hallway for a minute?"*

How an adult approaches and interacts with a student who is agitated can be the difference between a situation getting worse, or improving. Some people seem to just be good at knowing how to make things better. Sadly, there are those who seem to possess either a mean-streak or those who have an inability to de-escalate. Both result in adding to the problem rather than "right-sizing it". When a student has a chance to shift his or her perception through helpful intervention, it tends to reduce the distress. Below are the features, skills and know-how's needed to de-escalate situations:

## Tips That Will Help De-Escalate

√ Drop volume of your voice slightly below the student's level.

√ Remain calm and matter-of-fact; speak to the person, not the behavior.

√ Subdue quick or exaggerated gestures, particularly with arms and hands.

√ Stay cognizant of your "buttons"; respond rather than react.

√ Avoid having an audience of other students; people often perform for their peer group.

√ If you are angry, wait to interact until you are more objective (if at all possible).

√ Give choices to the student; it is empowering. Being helpless does not improve behavior.

√ Respect student's physical boundaries; stand about three feet apart.

√ Utilize active listening skills such a paraphrasing, summarizing, eye contact, etc.

√ Don't personalize what the student is doing.

## How Close is too Close?

People have about an eighteen-inch buffer zone that is in place for protection. When two are talking, the combined distance of comfort is about three feet. Anytime someone violates this space, people get uncomfortable (unless person was invited) and either step back or turn to the side.

## When De-escalating a Situation:

Do not get too close; it will add to the student's anxiety.
Avoid quick and unexpected gestures.
Make appropriate eye contact.

## Don't Forget

At birth, aren't we all good? When we see an infant, we do not think of words like, "incorrigible, delinquent, up to no good or trouble-maker". Somewhere along the way, kids are emotionally wounded and battered; some get physically battered. Defenses emerged for self-protection, and often take the form of acting out behavior. Remember, when we consider all that a students goes through (the known and unknown), it probably makes some sense he or she is acting out. There may be valid reasons that explain the behavior, but making excuses avoids accountability.

Anyone who works with young people has certain "buttons". What re-stimulates one teacher may mean little to another colleague. Self-awareness is key to not letting your buttons get pushed.

See the person and behavior as separate; one can actively confront the behavior while still supporting the student. Instead of the student being a bad kid, we have a kid who is exhibiting bad behavior.

Investing in developing skills for de-escalating a situation will provide dividends for a lifetime—not just for the student, but for you as well. Remember, it isn't a time factor that keeps adults from approaching interventions with compassion, it is an attitude factor. It really does not take any more time to intervene with care than with malice.

## Surely, There Must be Better Way?

"Who cares what you think; you're not my mother!" The classroom suddenly gets quiet; students are waiting to see how you respond. In a calm and measured voice you say, 'Sherry, can you step out in the hall with me for a moment? With reluctance, she responds, "I guess so. I didn't do anything, so why are you picking on me?" You don't respond to the hook.

In the hallway, you make eye contact with Sherry and start by saying, "You've been in my class all this time and this is the first time I've heard you talk that way. Is there something going on today?" Sherry shrugs her shoulders shakes her head and denies anything. You continue; "You've been a good student all year and all of the sudden I see a big change. There is something that is troubling you. I don't know what it is, but if you want, we can talk after class and right now go back in and carry on with the day. Or, you can see your counselor right now to talk with him. What do you prefer?"

"I don't know; I don't even know what to say. I'm sorry for what I said to you. Can we talk after class?" You respond with a matter-of-fact, "Sure we can. I would like that! In the mean time let's go back to class and agree not to repeat what happened in class earlier. Okay?" "Yes, thanks for not going off on me for doing that. I figured I was in for a screaming session with you." You make note of this comment for when you speak after class. Your final words at this time are, "Sherry, I'll always work with you to do what is needed to succeed in my class. Between the two of us, we can deal with a lot. I can't do this by myself. Can I get an agreement that we'll work together on your success?"

## Sound Corny? Try it and see what happens!

In conversations with kids, there are times when a comment is made that imply there is much more to the story. Sherry stated that she expected her teacher to scream at her. Apparently, she is being screamed at elsewhere. If this was counseling or therapy, the logical step would be to find out more about this by asking Sherry what is being said between the lines. When intervening, it is important not to get too far off center. The immediate goal is to address and interrupt the behavior. More can be discussed with the student in the future.

*"In nature we never see anything isolated, but everything in connection with something else which is before it, beside it, under it, and over it."*
**Johann Wolfgang von Goethe**

## It's about the Relationship

In a teacher's handbook, titled," *Discipline with Love*", learning was broken down to three primary areas of influence. It was determined that each of these three areas contributed to a student's learning in vastly different amounts.

## Three Primary Influences

The curriculum/teacher presentation style
(6%)
Factors the school has no control
(16%)
The relationship between student and teacher
(78%)

College degree, teacher certification, educational acts, research and focus tend to apply to the first area of influence. Local, state and federal policy-makers place the spotlight on curriculum and teacher qualifications, almost to the point of overshadowing the other two areas pertinent to learning. Schools have no control over the home environment, level of healthcare, quality of nutrition, or amount of sleep a child gets. The school cannot control the family's value system regarding education, the parents' marital status or work schedule.

Most adults can think back to a particular teacher we wanted to please, possibly a teacher that made learning exciting. This teacher wasn't necessarily the strictest or the most lenient. It had nothing to do with gender, age or ethnicity. This teacher somehow made you feel important, like you were valued in the class. This teacher had a way of making students feel important. It could have been good eye contact, a sense of humor, fairness in decisions, energy level, and interest in others, spontaneity or many other factors that made this teacher special. As a student, these factors really didn't matter so much. You just liked this teacher and this teacher liked you.

## Why Bring This Up?

Though the quality of the relationship between a teacher and student is vital, there clearly needs to be a curriculum and teaching style to consider as well. No matter how high the academic standards are though, the relationship cannot be ignored. The vast amount of learning is attributed to the quality of the relationship between student and teacher. Wouldn't it make sense if a teacher's ability to redirect behavior or manage a classroom was determined by similar factors? Can it be the stronger the relationship, the better the classroom management? With a good relationship, a teacher can make mistakes, overstep the process and practically fall on his face and still see a student respond well. How does a teacher establish a good relationship with a student? Even trying to respond to that question brings up so many variables and indirect factors; there is no way to give one answer. However, there are some basic tenets that are worth listing.

## Nurturing Classroom

While facilitating an in-service training for a school, I was referring to the belief that a positive, solution-focused approach gets better results when intervening with students. In the front of the room, a hand went up and an intolerant sounding voice exclaimed, *"We don't have time for that touchy-feely crap!"* For a moment the room was silent as I tried to figure out a response that could counter the comment, yet not embarrass or shame the speaker. Before I could even begin to formulate some kind of response, a voice from the back of the room responded, *"It doesn't take any more time to be caring than it takes to be a jerk!"* The room broke out in spontaneous applause. What a perfect answer to a very cynical comment.

## Cool Qualities

Accept individual differences.
Strive for a relaxed atmosphere.
All feelings are okay, but not all behaviors.
Separate person from behavior when confronting.
Allow students some control and choices over the day.
Promote a feeling of openness; it is okay to talk about problems.
Be respectful when redirecting behavior and giving consequences.
Help students view mistakes as normal part of learning.
Be an honest role model. Let students know how you feel about their behaviors.
Have clear, consistent, yet flexible rules versus inconsistent and rigid guidelines.

# Classroom Management Inventory

## Rate Your Classroom Disciplinary Practices
## This is very subjective and calls for honest self-examination.

Begin by placing a check in the appropriate column after each item.

| | Behavior | Usually | Sometimes | Never |
|---|---|---|---|---|
| 1. | I make sure to get students' attention before giving instructions. | ❑ | ❑ | ❑ |
| 2. | I set long term goals and refer to these when daily planning. | ❑ | ❑ | ❑ |
| 3. | When students are on task, I avoid interrupting them. | ❑ | ❑ | ❑ |
| 4. | I moderate my voice; avoid it being too fast or too high pitched. | ❑ | ❑ | ❑ |
| 5. | I set clear time limits for task completion. | ❑ | ❑ | ❑ |
| 6. | I circulate among students at work. | ❑ | ❑ | ❑ |
| 7. | I post classroom rules & guidelines. | ❑ | ❑ | ❑ |
| 8. | I quickly learn and use all student names. | ❑ | ❑ | ❑ |
| 9. | I am careful not to introduce too many topics simultaneously. | ❑ | ❑ | ❑ |
| 10. | I stick with time constraints and don't stretch out activities. | ❑ | ❑ | ❑ |
| 11. | I am consistent in what I say and do. | ❑ | ❑ | ❑ |
| 12. | I address bullying behavior every time I witness it (classroom, hallway, cafeteria). | ❑ | ❑ | ❑ |
| 13. | I think through instructions I will give to students. | ❑ | ❑ | ❑ |
| 14. | I am aware of the effects of my dress, voice, and movements on student behavior. | ❑ | ❑ | ❑ |
| 15. | I interact with all students and don't show favorites. | ❑ | ❑ | ❑ |
| 16. | I move around in class. | ❑ | ❑ | ❑ |

| | Usually | Sometimes | Never |
|---|---|---|---|
| **17.** I communicate positive expectations of good behavior to my class. | ☐ | ☐ | ☐ |
| **18.** I have clear and specific rules that I teach my students. | ☐ | ☐ | ☐ |
| **19.** I include humor in my teaching when possible. | ☐ | ☐ | ☐ |
| **20.** I consistently follow through with consequences to enforce rules. | ☐ | ☐ | ☐ |
| **21.** I am animated when teaching, aware of my expressions and body language. | ☐ | ☐ | ☐ |
| **22.** When possible, I reprimand students one-on-one, without other students observing. | ☐ | ☐ | ☐ |
| **23.** I respond to appropriate behavior with specific, personal praise. | ☐ | ☐ | ☐ |
| **24.** I avoid using threats to control students. | ☐ | ☐ | ☐ |
| **25.** I model honest communication, using feeling words, even when negative. | ☐ | ☐ | ☐ |
| | | | |

Then add your points—allowing 4 points for each "Usually," 2 points for each "Sometimes," and 0 points for each "Never" Now add the three numbers for a total.

**Rate yourself as follows:**

90-100 = Excellent

80-89 = Good

70-79 = Fair

below 70 = Poor

Adapted from National Education Association's *"I Can Do It"* Classroom Management training module, developed by *California Teachers Association.* For more information about this program, contact NEA Teacher Quality at (202) 822-7333. *Copyright © by the California Teachers Association. Republished with permission.*

*"I'm a good kid who has done bad things."*
**Michael B.**

## A List of Responsive Choices

The following is a list of eclectic ideas that are helpful when dealing with student behavior. Like a cafeteria, go down the line and choose what you like.

## Welcome and Come In

A middle school I worked with in central Texas reduced discipline referrals by more than 80% in one year. The primary strategy was to have the teachers greet the students at the classroom door, using their names. The students were given the choice to shake hands, bump knuckles or high five. The teachers were given an opportunity to connect with the students.

## Apology when Wrong

Apologies are one way that humans repair the social fabric after a conflict. The student may be asked to apologize to the offended party (e.g., teacher, students, principal) in writing or in person. It is important, though; that the offending student accept blame for the incident and demonstrate authentic regret in offering the apology, or neither party will be satisfied with the outcome.

## Behavioral Contract

The student and teacher hammer out a written agreement that outlines specific positive behaviors that the student is to engage in (or specific negative behavior that he or she is to avoid), the privileges or rewards that the student will earn for complying with the behavioral contract, and the terms by which the student is to earn the rewards.

## Loss of privileges

The student is informed in advance that he or she can access a series
of privileges (e.g., access to games to play, the opportunity to have five
minutes of free time) if his or her behavior remains appropriate. The
instructor instructs the student about what kind and the intensity of
problem behavior that may result in the loss of privileges, and for how
long. After this introductory phase, the instructor withdraws privileges, as
agreed upon, whenever the student misbehaves.

## Modeling (Vicarious Learning)

While the target student is observing, the teacher gives specific public
praise to children other than the target student when they show appropriate
behaviors. When praising these behaviors, the teacher clearly describes the
praiseworthy behaviors. When the target student "imitates" the same or
similar appropriate behaviors, the teacher immediately praises him or her.

## Parent contact

The teacher calls, sends a note home to, or e-mails the student's parent(s)
regarding the behavioral problems. The parent may be asked for advice
on how the teacher can better reach and teach the child at school. The
teacher may offer suggestions for appropriate parent involvement (e.g.,
"You may want to talk with your child about this incident, which we view
as serious.")

## Praise

When the student engages in a positive behavior that the teacher has selected
to increase, the teacher praises the student for that behavior. Along with
positive comments (e.g., "Great job!"), the praise statement should give
specifics about the behavior the child demonstrated that is being singled
out for praise ("You really kept your attention focused on me during that
last question, even when kids around you were talking.")

## Private approach

The instructor quietly approaches the student, points out the problem behavior and how it is interfering with class work or interrupting instruction. The instructor reminds the student of the academic task in which he or she should be engaged. The student is given an opportunity to explain his or her actions. The student is politely offered the choice to improve the behavior or accept a negative consequence.

## Promise

The instructor approaches the misbehaving student and informs him or her that the student has behaved inappropriately. The teacher asks the student to state an appropriate alternative behavior that he or she should have followed. The teacher then requests that the student promise the instructor (verbally or in writing) that he or she will not engage in this misbehavior again.

## Redirection

The teacher interrupts problem behavior by calling on the student to answer a question, assigning him or her task to carry out, or otherwise refocusing the child's attention.

## Reflective Essay

The student is required to write and submit to the teacher a brief composition after displaying behaviors. At minimum, the composition would state: (1) what problem behaviors the student displayed, (2) how the student could have acted in an alternative, more acceptable manner, and, (3) a promise from the student to show appropriate behaviors in similar situations in the future. NOTE: Some teachers use a pre-printed structured questionnaire containing these three items for the student to complete.

# Reprimand

In the typical reprimand, the instructor approaches the student, states that the student is misbehaving, and instructs the student to stop the behavior immediately. Reprimands should be used sparingly, as students may become defiant if confronted by an angry teacher in a public manner. When used, reprimands should be kept short, to avoid arguments with the student.

# Restitution

The student engages in an activity that actually or symbolically restores the environment, setting, or social situation that his or her misbehavior had damaged. For example, a student who marks up a wall with graffiti may be required to work after school under supervision of custodial staff to wash the wall and remove the offending markings.

# Rewarding Alternative (positive) Behaviors

The instructor calls on the student or provides other positive attention to incentives only during those times the student is showing appropriate social and academic behaviors. The same positive attention or consequences are withheld during times when the student misbehaves or does not engage in academics.

# Timeout/Detention/In-school Suspension

The student is removed from the classroom because of a behavioral infraction. In timeout, the student's exclusion from the classroom may be very short (3-5 minutes). With in-school suspension, the student may be removed from instruction for longer periods (e.g., half a day). Detention may require that the student spend time in a non-rewarding setting but that consequences may be deferred until after school to prevent loss of learning.

*Two monologues do not make a dialogue."*
**Jeff Daly**

## Dispute Resolution

Disputes arise because of perceived differences in interests. That is, if there is an interaction between two or more students, and one person believes that his or her interests are not met, there is often a dispute. Disputes can easily arise when students do not know each other well, when they are playing, or when there is a misunderstanding. Misunderstanding one another seems to be the most common reason for disputes. Without mediation, disputes often are "resolved in any of the following ways:

- One of the students gives in and lets the other student "win".
- An adult settles the situation and decides the outcome of the argument.
- The misunderstanding is recognized and there is no longer a reason to argue.
- One of the students is able to see the other student's side and decides stop arguing.
- An ongoing resentment flourishes or a fight occurs.

## Mediation

Most disputes between students are relatively simple, and do not call for formal mediation. Formal mediation includes more sophisticated and drawn out steps such as negotiation and arbitration. It often applies to adult situations such as divorce, land dispute, employee dispute and financial dispute.

I train adolescents to serve as peer mediators, expecting them to learn the step-by-step process. The goal is to keep it simple and short. Because of time constraints on many adults, the goal here is to present the steps in a similar manner. If I wrote this text as part of a formal mediation course, these steps would be much more thorough. However, these work well.

# Mediation Steps

- Arrange seating so that disputants are able to make eye contact with everyone.
- Explain confidentiality—"Everything that is said in here will stay in here. It will be kept private, except if you talk about hurting yourself, another person or you talk about someone hurting you".
- Explain that you will remain impartial and the solutions will come from the disputants.
- Present the rules of mediation:
  o **No name calling or put downs**
  o **Tell the truth**
  o **Don't interrupt the person speaking**
  o **Work to solve the problem**
- Get agreement—"Can you agree to these rules?"

## Beginning the mediation process

Both students need to tell his or her side of the story without interruption. Make sure each follow the rules. When the rules are not being followed, remind the person(s) of the stated guidelines. As a mediator, you are the one to make sure the meeting goes as planned.

1. Select one person to tell his or her side of the story first (coin toss, etc).
2. After he or she has shared, mediator summarizes—"so what you are saying is . . ."
3. Other person tells his or her side of the story.
4. Mediator summarizes.
5. Mediator asks if anyone wants to add more information.
6. If so, mediator summarizes.
7. Mediator tries to point out anything in common between the two.
8. Mediator asks both parties to make suggestions.
9. If suggestions are made, mediator asks for an agreement.
10. If suggestions are not made, remind students about the agreement to "work to solve the problem", and ask both students what the

other student might need to do in order for the dispute to be resolved.

11. If needed, mediator asks both students to predict what will probably happen, if a resolution is not reached.

12. After each have commented, mediator offers one more opportunity to come up with suggestions.

13. If made, mediator summarizes and wraps up the meeting with an agreement from both.

14. If students still will not work to solve the problem, the mediator announces that the meeting is over and wraps up with a word of encouragement, as well as a caution about the predictions.

The mediation is finished. However, there are times when this process does not bring about resolution. Reasons mediation may not work include:

- Only one of the students wanted to resolve the dispute.
- The students interrupted each other.
- The student(s) felt he or she was not listened to.
- The mediator appeared to take sides.
- Something deeper exists that was not discussed in the process. One or both of the students might need to see a counselor.

## Word of Caution

Mediation works when there is equal power between the two students. Asking the target of bullying to meet with the bully for mediation is like asking you to mediate with the burglar who just robbed your house. There is no compromise sought. One of the students is simply wrong. No student who has been terrorized by a bully should have to sit facing him or her. Bullies need to be addressed very differently, which will be covered in Chapter 21.

## More Than Two Students

Disputes can grow to include friends on both sides, resulting in a situation where one group is in dispute with another. Experience suggests that mediating two opposing groups is not a good idea. There are too many voices, opinions, reactions, etc. Kids may posture for peers, coming across more arrogant, resistant and flippant. Keep mediation between two people, even if the two represent groups. Remember, it is getting the two sides to sense that his or her interests are met. With more than two in the mediation, the interests are wide and varying, making it very difficult to appease all who are participating.

The following is a example scenario of a teacher mediating with two boys who need assistance. Sample dialogue can always be sanitized to the point that it loses pertinence. Not all mediations work, however when they do, it looks a lot like the following.

## Boys Hallway Conflict

Set Up: Two eighth grade boys get into an argument in your class. This argument includes aggressive posturing and verbal threats, with both boys pushing each other. There was no hitting and you were able to interrupt before anything worse occurred. Without intervention and resolution, the chance of this argument continuing in the hallway or cafeteria is substantial. Both the boys are good students. They both take your class serious and often eager to help. You break up the confrontation and ask both boys to sit down and remain after class. In a matter of fact tone of voice, you ask both boys to stay behind after class for a few minutes. You offer the boys an opportunity to work out the dispute through mediation. After explaining the process, both agree and make plans to see you tomorrow after the last period.

Teacher: My job is to not take sides or be the one to come up with solution. That will be your job to do. Does that make sense?

Terry: What if we can't come up with anything?

Teacher: Let's see what happens first.

Jonah: Fine! Can we just get started?

Teacher: The purpose of mediation is to help you two resolve the conflict. I'm not here to decide who is right or wrong. Instead, I hope you can do what is called a win-win, with both of you thinking things are better. I have four basic ground rules that need to be agreed upon. They are, no name calling, no interruptions, tell the truth, and agree to work to solve the problem. Can both of you accept and follow these rules?

Jonah: I can if he can!

Terry: Whatever!

Teacher: I need a yes or no from both of you.

Terry Yeah, I mean yes mam!

Jonah: Sure!

Teacher: Good! Now let's start by deciding who goes first. I'm going to flip a coin with heads for Terry and tails for Jonah. It is tails. Jonah, tell me your side of the story.

Jonah: Cool! I was talking with Sylvia Saucedo after 3rd period when this dude comes up and goes crazy shoving me and yelling. He tells me to stay away from his girlfriend or he'll kick my butt. I told him I'd talk to anyone I wanted to and would happily kick his right back.

Terry: Like you could.

Teacher: Terry, you agreed to not interrupt. Let's remember the rules. Go on with your side, Jonah.

Jonah: Then the bell rang and we went to 4th period. Yesterday in the hallway, he came up to me again talking all kinds of crap about stomping my face in. Then in your class and he gave me "the look", so I said something back.

Teacher: What you are saying is you were talking with a girl in the hallway between classes, and Terry came up to you making threats. Later, Terry again came up saying something about wanting to fight. Then in my class, it continued. Is that right?

Jonah: Pretty much! Don't forget the part about me not taking his crap.

Teacher: All right Terry, now it is your time to tell your side of the story.

Terry: I can't wait! Man, I was going to my locker after 3rd period when I saw this dude hanging all over Sylvia. She's my girlfriend, man. It looked like she was having a hard time getting away so I pushed him away. I did tell him to back off or I'd do some damage. He got all cocky and claimed I'd regret trying it. If that bell hadn't rung, we probably would have thrown right then and there. In the hallway, I see him hassling her again. Man, there is one thing my father taught me and that was to protect what is mine.

Jonah: Man, she isn't yours. You think she's property or something?

Teacher: Again, you need to remember the rules about interrupting.

Terry:      First of all, I don't think of her as property. All I meant is that
            I protect my girlfriend. Anyway, after I saw him with her, I got
            mad and came up and shoved him hard. He pushed me back.
            Before it got bad, the bell rang and we came to your class.

Teacher:    What you are saying is you were going to your locker after 3rd
            period, saw him with your girlfriend and told him to back off.
            You wanted to protect her from being hassled. After warning
            Jonah, you saw him again talking to her. This time you came up
            and pushed him. In turn, he pushed you. That's when the bell
            rang and you came to my class. Right?

Terry:      That sums it up!

Teacher:    The next thing is I want to offer both of you the chance to add
            anything more to your side. Is there anything else Jonah?

Jonah:      Heck yeah! I wasn't hurting her. I wasn't even trying to really
            talk with her. Look, Sylvia's locker is next to mine. I was having
            trouble closing it because I keep it messy. I leaned hard with my
            shoulder and slipped, falling into her. I was apologizing when
            he comes up talking all bad and tough. I didn't know what he
            was talking about. All I know is he threatened and shoved me.
            What was I supposed to do, let him get away with it? Then in the
            hallway, I saw Sylvia and went to ask her where he was. I wanted
            to explain things, but before I had the chance, he comes up again
            and pushes me hard, in front of everyone in. I had no choice but
            to push back.

Teacher:    You are saying that you accidentally fell into Sylvia while trying
            to close your locker and when you were apologizing to her, Terry
            came up and things got out of hand quickly. Then in the hallway,
            you asked Sylvia where Terry was so you could explain. But,
            before getting the chance, the two of you starting yelling and
            shoving. Is that accurate?

Jonah:      That's how it happened! If he wasn't so stupid, we wouldn't have
            gotten in trouble.

Teacher:    You agreed not to insult each other. In order for mediation to
            work, you need to follow these rules. I noticed while you both
            were telling your side, that you didn't seem to have a conflict
            before today. You also seem to have something else in common,
            which is you both have pride and a strong sense of standing up
            for yourself. Is that correct?

Terry: I guess? I never really thought about us having things in common. Hey man, why didn't you say something when I first came up? I thought you were making a move on her. I flew off the handle when I saw you in the hallway. I couldn't believe you were disrespecting me like that. Instead of thinking, I reacted.

Jonah: Dude, I wanted to say something, but before I could start, you offered to rearrange my face. After that, I didn't want to explain anything.

Teacher: Let me summarize what's been said so far. While Jonah was attempting to apologize for falling into Sylvia, Terry threatened and pushed you. Later in the hallway, Jonah asked Sylvia where you were Terry, so an explanation could be made. Again, things got out of hand again. It sounds like you both had some misunderstanding. Terry misunderstood why Jonah was up against your girlfriend. And, Jonah misunderstood why Terry was threatening and pushing you. Both of you made assumptions. It sounds like before this, neither of you had a problem with the other. Let's see if you guys have some answers or suggestions. What are some ideas?

Terry: I guess I can check things out before jumping to conclusions.

Jonah: Me too.

Teacher: If you don't work this out now, what do you two think might happen next?

Terry: We'll probably end up doing something stupid like fighting and get suspended from school.

Jonah: Not only that, but we'd end up fighting over something stupid. If I'm going to get kicked out of school, it better be for a good reason; not a misunderstanding!

Teacher: What could you do next time that would keep something like this from getting out of hand?

Jonah: Do a better job of explaining myself, instead of jumping to fight.

Terry: I can check things out before acting. Instead of immediately wanting to fight, I can first see what's up.

Teacher: It sounds like you both jumped to conclusions and wanted to fight each other. Once you found out the truth, neither seems ready to fight. Is that right?

Jonah: Yeah!

Terry:      Pretty much!

Teacher:  So Jonah, do you agree to the suggestions about checking things out first?

Jonah:    Yep.

Teacher:  How about you Terry, do you agree?

Terry:      Sure, it's no big deal.

Teacher:  Great! The way we end this mediation is to get you guys to make an agreement and give your word that you will keep it. If you remember, your agreement is to do a better job of explaining yourself and check things out before jumping to conclusions. I want to thank you for taking this mediation serious and working to solve the problem. You'll notice that I did not make any suggestions. The solution came from both of you. Good job! I will see you both in class tomorrow. By the way, don't forget we are having a test.

A good mediation is an excellent form of intervention. Being able to mediate when the opportunity arises not only addresses the behavior, but puts students in charge of coming up with the solutions. This kind of empowerment is good for kids, it fosters responsibility, accountability and ownership of behavior.

## To Understand

To understand is not enough
To recognize the toxicity
And grasp the reason for failure
Understanding breeds empathy

What good is knowledge untested?
Insights and intuition abound with eager expectations
Waiting to emerge from self-imposed binding
It is good to understand; it is not enough

Take what you know and go beyond
New learning brings answers and fuels concerns
Concerns provide the spark for the flame
This fire burns inside you, for the known and the hidden

The message and the methods are here
The efforts abide in your hands
Essential that our children flourish
Self-evident; well known

Another tool to help you reach out
Take what you know and move on
Change a life, even if just one
The longest road begins with just one brick

Is it your efforts, or the connections?
Is it what you hand them, or is it how you hand it?
The warmth of sunlight melts the coldest ice
The quality of the relationship is unequaled

Be centered on the person, not the actions
Learn new ways to help
Recognize there are good reasons
Let insight light the way

The results may amaze and your efforts reward
Some will thrive and others will whither
One must agree that it is important to say
I did my best; I could not do more

*"The mediocre teacher tells. The good teacher explains. The superior teacher demonstrates. The great teacher inspires."*
**William Arthur Ward**

# Chapter 17

## Great Teachers

What constitutes a great teacher is at times so abstract that it is hard to capture in writing. Personality, style, experience, insight and technique all come together in a confluence of factors that mix in different proportions. Then there is the x-factor, that special something that a teacher has that makes him or her great. However, being a good teacher is not an accident and is worthy of an attempt to include the components.

### Thank You, Mrs. Arnold!

Mrs. Arnold was tall, broad shouldered and carried a commanding voice. She taught 10$^{th}$ grade English and had a way of running her class that resulted in very little acting out. One of those rare moments had to do with me. Thankfully, you'll see, her intervention skills shifted the direction I was taking.

What made my experience in her class so valuable was fostered the previous year. My freshman English teacher was a tyrant. She was mean-spirited, carried a chip on her shoulder, and targeted certain people in class. She bullied her students and appeared to care little about the learning that went on in class. She intimidated her students by demanding respect; power was her primary tool of classroom management.

Pertinent to this story is a quick look at my family. My father was on the local City Council for two terms and was somewhat notorious and well known; his name was Dan. Prior to politics, both my parents were in television and hosted a daytime show at noon. The show featured local events, talents or people. My parents were well known.

When she wanted my attention, Ms. Bane would snap her fingers and bark, *"Dan Love's little boy, get up here."* Why she referred to me the way she did was her way of showing me that it didn't matter who my father was, she was the authority that counted. It is important to know that I never even once made reference to my father in front of her, and neither of my parents would ever have tried to tell her how to teach. In those days, the teacher was always right and parents always supported her.

One day, Ms. Bane in front of the class said in a loud condescending voice, *"Little boy, your number is #6595"*. I asked her what that was and she arrogantly announced to all that it was my *"prison number"*. Even some of the other students gasped at her style. When asked why she said that, Ms. Bane retorted; *"Just look at you!"* I looked down in confusion and saw a pair of sandals on my feet. I wore the sandals without socks which was a violation of the school's dress code. I was a rule breaker. Earlier that week, I'd smashed my big toe and the scab kept sticking to my sock. For that, I was issued a prison number. That's not all!

All year it continued; she'd treat me with a loathing more appropriate for someone caught stealing. My grades began slipping and on a final exam she gave me a zero, claiming she couldn't tell my T's (true) from my F's (false). I ended up failing freshman English. She seemed to take pleasure in my failure. I went to summer school and got caught up. I would enter the new school year in good standing, with head held high and arms crossed defiantly. No one would dare do to me what was done last year. I had a chip on a shoulder waiting to be knocked off.

Where Ms. Bane was insensitive, shaming and sometimes a bully, my 10th grade English teacher was a savior; I just wasn't aware at first. I'm convinced that the following incident changed the course of my life.

At the beginning of the school year, in her classroom a friend leaned over and quietly offered me chewing tobacco. First of all, I didn't chew and second of all, I had no place to spit. Being a sixteen-year-old boy with an attitude, I put a plug in my mouth. I was somewhat lacking in forethought. Well the tobacco grew and swelled in my mouth, threatening to come bursting out with tobacco juice trickling through my sealed lips.

I had two options, swallow or spit. I chose to spit on Mrs. Arnold's floor. It really was no contest. I leaned back and let a steady stream drip out of my mouth right on her tile floor. Thinking I was being inconspicuous, I dropped the remaining plug into the middle of a horrible and nasty brown puddle.

At some point in class Mrs. Arnold walked down the isle and inquired in a worried voice, *"Oh my, what happened here?"* It wasn't an accusing statement; she seemed to genuinely want to know how the brown puddle got on her floor. I lied, *"Oh, Mrs. Arnold, it was here when I came in but I didn't want to tell you because you might throw up. I was going to clean it for you!"* A sixteen year old boy offering to clean up someone else's mess: yah right! Her next comment blew me away.

*"Noel Love (she used my own name), you are one of the nicest young men I've had in my classroom; you are a pleasure to teach. Thank you!"* She walked away. My shame and guilt seeped out like a broken sewer. I wanted to call her back; I wanted to confess my transgressions. I kept quiet, wiped my sweaty brow and sighed relief. I had gotten away with it. It was never mentioned again. I wasn't able to forget it either.

I excelled in her class. I thrived in English and took it as an elective my junior and senior year and in college tested out a year and a half early. I was good at English and had failed it in the ninth grade. One person can make a difference. Mrs. Arnold could easily have exacerbated the situation, and by all rights should have. Instead she did something that resulted in my dedication, gratitude and indebtedness to her and her classroom. I would live up to her comments. I would perform for her. I would be a pleasure to teach!

An intervention is when the behavior of concern is interrupted with the intent on leveraging positive decisions or changes. Sadly, many interventions occur because of crisis, where there is no planning or preparation. Interventions can precede a crisis and get the same results and it begs us to ask why this is not done more often. When not done early, we see increased discipline referrals, suspensions, expulsions and alternative campuses. In society, we see bulging jails, a huge increase in prisons, overburdened probation officers and a lot of damaged young lives. Effective interventions are not only altruistically called for; they save money by heading off a problem before it gets worse.

For years, I intended to drop by her class and let Mrs. Arnold know how she profoundly influenced my life. I wanted to thank her. Before this happened, I read her name in the obituaries. Lamenting to a friend about my regret in not acting sooner, he said, "Maybe she knew how you felt." Explain I said. "By doing so well in her class . . . . you, let her know." "Maybe", I said. "I would have liked to look her in the eyes and tell her how she threw a life preserver to a kid who didn't even know he was drowning."

Over the years, I have asked educators and students in my workshops what qualities their favorite teacher possessed. Teachers attending training consistently list the following characteristics:

## Teacher Qualities

| | |
|---|---|
| Consistent | Genuine |
| Passionate | Motivating |
| Excited to teach | Take action |
| Encouraging to all | Cooperative |
| Prepared every day | Use word "yes" |
| Clear communicator | Expect the best |
| Entertaining and fun | Respectful to class |
| Organized and ready | Reinforce the positive |
| Interested in students | Encourage self-control |
| Humorous personality | Build children's images |
| Reliable on daily basis | Focus on the desired behavior |
| Enthusiastic educator | Clear and consistent directions |

These accolades are a composite and not intended to represent one particular teacher. Instead, they are offered as a reminder that students do have a clear idea of what a good teacher is and what to expect.

Consistency seems to stand out as a key to a teacher's effectiveness. Knowing what to expect from day to day is in itself a foundation in which learning can occur.

## Guiding Values

When addressing behavior, the following values of positive intervention are important. This information is taken from an article *Teacher Strategies That Encourage Responsive Students* by Suzanne Pitner,

1. Students want to do the right thing. Students do not want to be in trouble, or be embarrassed in front of their peers. Rather, they want recognition for a job well done, as most people do. A teacher can build on this desire by having faith in the students and setting positive expectations.
2. Be specific when giving directions and when giving praise. Instead of saying "Don't litter," say "Please put all your snack trash in the garbage can." The compliment "Good job," is vague. A more

effective form of praise is to say, "I appreciate how you picked up the trash you saw in the hallway."

3. Direct your focus on one student at a time. Pull the student aside for guidance in a one to one situation, in a place where other students will not overhear. This prevents embarrassment and helps the student to respond to the guidance in an honest manner.

4. Don't talk too much. Young students have a short attention span, and can't remember long lists of instructions or comments. Keep instructions down to one or two steps. Have the students repeat the instructions to be sure they know what to do.

5. Give the students time to respond. This is especially true when working with English language learners, who may need additional time to process what you have said, and to develop their response. Wait for an answer when asking a question, and give them at least 20 seconds to reply. Don't interrupt, but rather, follow up with questions that encourage critical thinking and reasoning.

Using these five guidelines allows students to maintain dignity, and makes them willing to please the teacher. Part of a teacher's job is to guide a student, developing good thinking skills and social skills. Positive classroom discipline techniques help produce positive, happy students.

# The National Education Association offers the following techniques for maintaining control without confrontation

## Important Strategies

Once students are settled in the classroom, you will want to continue with some of these teacher-recommended techniques for maintaining control without confrontation:

1. Establish eye contact.
2. Move around the room and increase proximity to restless students.
3. Send a silent signal.
4. Give a quiet reminder.
5. Re-direct a student's attention.
6. Begin a new activity.
7. Offer a choice.
8. Use humor.
9. Provide positive reinforcement.
10. Wait quietly until everyone is on task.
11. Ask a directed question.

On the following pages, you will find a way to identify your qualities. This is very subjective and not meant to reveal anything you do not already know. It is good to see it in front of us in black and white.

## Your Character

| PERSONAL | CLASSROOM |
|---|---|
| Humble—Admits mistakes or errors when he/she makes them. | Prepared—Reviews lecture notes and examples to ensure they are current/correct. |
| Honest—Always tells students the truth about the situation and explains actions with reasons. | Organized—Has course syllabi with grading method explained on first day of class. |
| Discipline—Shows self-control and can be counted on to do the right thing in every situation. | Consistent—Teaches with no emotional outbreaks or unpredictable behavior patterns which intimidate students. |
| Compassionate—Shows he/she really cares about the student personally/professionally. | Work Ethic—Spends time to thoroughly prepare classes and laboratories. |
| Integrity—Always does what he/she says regardless of the consequences. | Prompt—Comes to class on time and does not run classes over allotted time. |
| Enthusiastic—Obviously believes in what he/she is teaching to include "living" it. | Flexible Attitude—Open to new ideas, suggestions and insights from students |
| Good Motive—Best interest of students is always No. 1 priority. | Interactive Dialogue—Classes are a two-way, meaningful communications experience. |
| Committed—Shows passion and zeal for teaching the subject material. | Learning environment—Encourages a casual and open setting vice a rigid/strict one |

# Your Competence

| |
|---|
| Possesses adequate academic and professional credentials. |
| Has actual experience in the application of course material to real life situations. |
| Has a definite command of the subject material exhibited in his/her confidence level. |
| Offers examples from a variety of sources to support course content. |
| Remains current in his/her field through active consulting and continuing education. |
| Demonstrates excellent communications skills and understands the "art" of communicating. |
| Handles students' questions with ease and does not consider questions as threatening. |
| Maintains vibrant relationships with academic and professional colleagues through attendance at and participation in various activities. |

## Your Connections to Students

| Items | Items |
|---|---|
| Learn student's name and address them with it | Show excitement and enthusiasm for teaching |
| Develop your listening skills/take class in it | Always encourage students |
| Be available for formal/informal office hours | Talk at student's level and seek feedback |
| Trust that I have the ability and desire to learn | Remember students have hopes and dreams |
| Use humor and be humorous when possible | Actively engage students with questions |
| Share stories of/about yourself as a student | Be positive and don't criticize students |
| Smile!—A great non-verbal that says a lot | Be an advisor to at least one student group |
| Use some collaborative learning so students can get to know each other better | Discuss real life professional successes and failures and what you learned from them |
| Show respect and be courteous to students | Appeal to student's sense of pride and worth |

Robert Martinazzi and Jerry Samples [(2000). *Characteristics and traits of an effective professor.* ASEE/IEEE Frontiers in Education Conference. Kansas City, MO.]

*"You don't catch a bass with bait for a trout"*
**Anonymous**

# Chapter 18

# Interventions of a Different Flavor

Without question, the best way to incorporate a skill is to practice it. First, it helps to get a clear idea of what the skill looks like. The first example is a classroom teacher intervening with a specific behavior. This is followed by an administrator and an early intervention team (SAP Core Team) example for you to read.

## Intervening in the Classroom

## Set Up

Andrew is in the 6th grade and currently in his science class. His teacher is being challenged to intervene with certain behaviors and attitudes. After twice ignoring Mr. Harris, Andrew is once more confronted and told to be quiet and sit down. He not only ignores his teacher but he says under his breath, *"Like you can make me!"* The students who are close to him hear this comment; Mr. Harris only hears a few words.

**Mr. Harris**: Stopping his explanation about igneous rocks, he says; *"Andrew I know we could do this all period long, but I doubt either of us really enjoys it"*.

**Andrew**: Snickering, he responds; *"I'm having a great time; this is fun and maybe I'll keep it up."*

**Mr. Harris**: Managing to not get hooked says; *"Well, that may be so. Would you come out in the hallway so you can continue to say what is on your mind? It will only take a few minutes."*

**Andrew:** Reluctantly and aware others are watching states; *"Whatever! If it will make you happy I'll step out. I don't want to be in this class anyway."*

**Mr. Harris**: *"I appreciate that; we'll go out here."* He walks out with Andrew, not saying anything else until in the hall. *"I get the impression that you aren't real interested in class today, is that so?"*

**Andrew**: Shrugging his shoulders, looks around and says; *"It's a bunch of crap; who needs to know about stupid rocks?"*

**Mr. Harris**: Not responding to the question states: *"I bet you aren't alone in how you feel about class. As a matter of fact I know other students who feel exactly like you do."*

**Andrew**: Acting apathetic he responds; *"Whatever, I guess that's cool. Maybe you should be talking with them instead of me."*

**Mr. Harris**: *"I can understand how you feel. I'm concerned that if you keep ignoring me when I ask you to do something you will eventually get into more trouble. I'm not talking about here in class, but somewhere else. I bet science isn't the only class you don't like."*

**Andrew**: *"You got that right; this whole school blows and no one likes being here. None of the teachers even like me anyway."*

**Mr. Harris**: *"You mean even with your teachers not liking you, you came to school anyway? I think that is pretty tough. Today seems even more frustrating to you than other days. Why is that?"*

**Andrew**: Looking down, *"It's no big deal. Who cares anyway; I sure don't."*

**Mr. Harris**: *"What is no big deal, Andrew?"*

**Andrew**: *"It's nothing! My dad moved out last night. It's supposed to be only for a while, but I know better."*

**Mr. Harris**: *"Look, with what you just told me, I'd like to give you a choice right now. I'd love you to come back to class and join in; or, if you want, I'll be more than happy to send you to the counselor. What do you want to do?"*

**Andrew**: Defiantly he says; *"Why talk about it? Nothing changes anyway. Nothing I do makes a difference."*

**Mr. Harris**: *"I hear you! If you are choosing to come back in with me, that would be great. I know how hard it is to come to school when it seems things are bad. Like I said earlier, I'm impressed you even came to school today with what you've told me."*

**Andrew**: *"I don't care. I might as well come back in and stay in your class."*

**Mr. Harris**: *"Okay, Andrew. Thanks for coming out and talking with me. It helps to know what you're going through."*

Upon re-entering the class, Andrew sat down and appeared to look bored. He did not interrupt Mr. Harris again. A connection was made that day that eventually resulted in a good relationship between Andrew and Mr. Harris. As the relationship improved, so did Andrew's behavior and attitude.

## Points to Consider and Remember

√ Considering all things, known and unknown about the student, the behavior that is presented usually makes sense. If we know all that the student is going through, we would realize that what we are seeing in the classroom is understandable. Ordinarily, it isn't about you. This does not imply it is acceptable.

√ Students can change behavior much easier than themselves. Generally kids do not see this separation. This statement applies to adults as well. In the classroom, it is the behavior that is the problem, not the child. A teacher can directly and thoroughly address inappropriate behavior and at the very same time support the individual. To not do so is to attack the person, which rarely achieves the goal of the intervention.

√ It must be recognized that adults have distress patterns as well that may get re-stimulated by the student behavior. Avoid responding to a student in an emotional manner. We respond best when we can think clearly.

√ It is the relationship between the teacher and student that influences the outcome of a classroom intervention more than all other factors. A strong relationship allows for a person's intervention skills to be awkward. Even if you have profound communication skills, but no relationship with the student, some of your intervention practices may fall short of the desired intent.

Where the classroom intervention is based on the relationship between student and teacher, and the skill level, the administrator intervention modeled next is based on the leverage of a discipline violation. The main intent is to use what happened as a way to encourage a willingness of the parents to take action. The incident alone is not sufficient and good communication skills are essential. In this next scenario, a grade level high school principal is meeting with the parents of a student who has been engaging in aggressive behavior that calls for alternative placement. You'll see that this principal thinks more can be done to help the student than alternative placement.

## Administrator Intervention

## Set up

Peter, a sixteen year old junior in high school received a discipline referral for the third time this semester. The previous referrals were for pushing and shoving in the halls between classes. This time, a teacher observed Peter slam a freshman against a locker and knee him in the crotch. Because of the frequency and severity of his behavior, Peter's mother and father were called and immediately came to school for a meeting. Peter joins the meeting after the parents and the principal have met.

**Principal:** Welcome Mrs. and Mr. Abernathy. I am Vera Cruz, Junior-level principal. I was the one who called you this morning. We need to talk about Peter and how he is doing at school. I know you've spoken with several of his teachers about his dropping grades, but this isn't why I called you today.

**Dad**: *What's the little loser done now?*

**Mom**: *"Oh honey, I asked you not to call him that, remember?"* Mom seems somewhat embarrassed and makes an expression that indicates that she is sorry.

**Dad:** Forcefully dad spews, *"That was before today. I'll call him what I want, when I want, where I want! Do you hear?"*

**Principal:** Remaining calm and matter-of-fact, *"This can be stressful and I understand it might be difficult. Is there anything I can get you that might help? Would you care for something to drink?*

**Dad**: *"Yeah! A strong drink wouldn't hurt!* He looks at mom and declares, *"I was just joking. Jeez honey, do you have to be so uptight?"*

**Principal:** Before mom can get pulled into a defensive mode, Mrs. Cruz quickly interjects, *"I'll have a soft drink or coffee brought in; what would you like?"* After a few seconds of no response, she continues, *"Well, if you change your mind, let me know. What happened today with Peter was part of a pattern* *that includes two other referrals for similar behavior.*" Looking at mom, "*I spoke with you both times I believe, Mrs. Abernathy?*

**Mom:** With a fearful expression she says to dad, "*Don't get mad; I didn't tell you because I didn't want you to worry. With work being stressful, I figured you didn't need to be bothered by something like this. I hope you aren't mad!*"

**Dad:** "*We'll discuss this at home in private. Now, on to the little loser. What are we supposed to do?*"

**Principal:** "*Because of this third referral, I am going to send Peter to our alternative campus for thirty days. He'll continue his school work, but will have to abide by some pretty strict rules in order to avoid a suspension.*" She looks at both anticipating an outburst.

**Dad:** "*So! Why should I care? I've about given up on the boy.*"

**Principal:** "*I'm going to have Peter join us and I want to be sure we are all clear on what is happening. But, before I do this, I want to ask you a question. Is the aggressive behavior a surprise to you?*"

**Mom:** Sheepishly and hesitantly she says, "*Well, kind of! I mean this school year is the first time Peter has ever gotten in trouble at school. Before that, he was a nice, sweet boy. Right, honey?*"

**Dad:** With a bored affect he answers: "*Yeah, I suppose so.*"

**Principal:** "*When we see a sudden or drastic change in a student's behavior, we try to ensure that the right things are done. What I mean is . . . I think Peter needs more help than the alternative school.*"

**Dad:** Exploding in his chair, "*There it is!* Looking at his wife, "*I told you they'd try and put him in the nut hut. That's what they do with everyone. My buddy at work told me about it . . . He warned me about you guys!*"

**Mom:** In a pleading voice, "*Let's at least listen to what she has to say. Quite frankly, I've been worried about Peter for a while now and I think it wouldn't hurt to let her talk.*"

**Principal**: *"All I was going to discuss was the possibility of you two agreeing to a confidential meeting with someone to discuss and assess what may be going on with Peter. There is no charge and we've had other parents take us up on this and it seems to help. If you are willing to follow through with this suggestion, I will work to shorten Peter's time at the ALC by one week. How does that sound?"*

**Mom:** Taking more charge of the conversation mom says, *"This is the first good thing we've heard today. What exactly are you talking about? Do you think Peter needs therapy? I think that is a bit out of your league, Mrs. Cruz. Let's not get too excited here. He's our son and we'll make these kinds of decisions."*

**Principal**: *"I agree one-hundred percent. I am not qualified to suggest Peter needs therapy and you have complete control on whether or not you choose to do this. I just want to help Peter with his grades and behavior. We all want this year to be successful, right?"* Both just shrug their shoulders.

**Principal**: Continuing, *"Let me explain what I was talking about. Is this okay?"* Both parents nod their approval. *"Adolescence is a tough time and things aren't the way they were when we were this age. There are so many things that can interfere and possibly hurt Peter's school work and how he feels about himself. His short temper and aggressive behavior suggest something is going on. We have several people in our town who offer their services to our parents at no charge. I need to be clear; if you want, we can help you set up a behavioral health assessment that can find, or rule out, what may be the underlying reasons for his behavior. It is free and is done off campus. Mr. and Mrs. Abernathy, we've had other students receive the assessment and it not only was kept private, but it helped the parents come up with some really good ideas. It does help."*

**Dad:** *"That was a mouthful. You're saying we can find out what is wrong with our son. Let's do it. No son of mine is going to fail school or get suspended."* He looks at mom and she agrees with relief.

**Principal**: Looking at mom, she asks, *"Mrs. Abernathy, what do you think?"*

**Mom:** With a sense of relief, she sighs, *"Oh yes! I've prayed every night for him. I just didn't know what to do. Being a parent of a teenager is tough. Even when things are okay, they are pretty hard to figure out. Let's schedule the meeting."*

## More Points to Consider

√ Do not get hooked into tangled emotions. The need for objectivity and detachment is high. Reacting to comments or pursuing tangents that are off target should be avoided.

√ Stay out of the dynamics between parents. Remaining neutral in this setting is absolutely needed. Even an appearance of bias changes the meeting.

√ Follow up at the end of the meeting by assisting parents with phone calls, etc. The more done immediately after the meeting, the better.

# Early Intervention Team or SAP Core Team Intervention

## The Set Up

Based on patterns of behavior displayed in the classroom, Jeremy James was referred to the SAP Core Team. This referral came after repeatedly failed attempts to redirect Jeremy's behavior. As a fourth-grade teacher, Ms. Loveless was well aware that her best efforts to redirect and re-engage Jeremy were not working. More and more, Ms. Loveless had been dealing with Jeremy's acting out behaviors that interfered with Jeremy and the other students' learning. Despite the consequences given, Jeremy continued the behaviors of concern, resulting in a vicious cycle. Every consequence given seemed to compound the behavior.

After completing a *behavior observation sheet*, Ms. Loveless placed it in the SAP box in the staff mailroom. Once received by the Core Team, further concerns were gathered from other teachers who work with Jeremy, along with information from permanent records, discipline files, attendance printout, and report cards.

The screening indicated that there was some kind of problem seen by more than one teacher. Without speculating about what was causing the behavior, the team determined that Jeremy had displayed an inability to redirect his own behaviors, despite the consequences given, and that the on-campus resources so far had not be effective. The recommendation that the team felt was most appropriate for Jeremy was to offer an behavioral assessment by one of the community services that volunteer their assessment services free of charge. A call was placed to Jeremy's mother and a meeting was scheduled for the next day. Mrs. James was informed that the meeting would last about 30 minutes and would be with Ms. Loveless, Jeremy's counselor and the school principal. When Mrs. James arrived at the school, she was offered some coffee and invited to sit in the conference room. (It is at this point where we will join this meeting, with an emphasis on the exchange between the members of the team and Mrs. James.)

**Principal**: Appearing relaxed and friendly, *"I want to thank you for coming in. As I indicated on the phone, this meeting should take about twenty to thirty minutes. Your son won't participate in this meeting, but he knows that you're here. Following this meeting, if you want to visit with him, I'll arrange it. I'd* *like to introduce you to the other two people who work with me. On your left is Mr. Smith, your son's counselor, and on the right, of course, is Judith Loveless, Jeremy's Language Arts teacher. Before we start, do you have any questions?"*

**Mom**: Looking very agitated, she says, *"Not really. I just hope this doesn't take too long. What's the little troublemaker done now?"* She slaps her hands down on the table and makes little eye contact.

**Principal**: Without reacting to the anger, *"We have a process at school called the Student Assistance Program that is very good at helping our students be successful. We know that some students experience difficulty and need assistance. We have what may be called traditional resources to help—guidance counselors, discipline referrals, nurses, and other services that help at times. Our primary concern at this point is that Jeremy has not responded to the attempts to help. The purpose of this meeting is to present exactly what all of Jeremy's teachers have observed, as well as other data that we have gathered. We've made copies of all this information so that you can review it at home. Most important is that we are here to help Jeremy succeed, and this meeting is our best effort. The other things we've tried this year have not worked as well as we had hoped. Our belief is that if we work in an alliance with parents, our chances for success increases. I hope that this meeting results in a continuation of that type of support for you and Jeremy. My role in this meeting is to keep us on track and make sure all of your questions are answered. Jeremy's counselor is going to share some information that we've gathered from our records and files and Ms. Loveless is going to present you with the classroom observations and concerns."*

**Mom**: Exasperated, she says, *"Look, I'm a single mother; I work late, and I have two other children besides Jeremy to look after. Can't you deal with this? Why do you need me to get involved?"* Her voice takes on a pleading tone.

**Principal**: *"Mrs. James, normally we try to deal with as much as we can, but once we realize that our best efforts have not succeeded, the situation suggests strongly that we try to get some help from the parent. Toward the end of this meeting, we are going to give you some recommendations that we think could be very helpful. At this point I am going to turn things over to Mr. Smith."*

**Counselor**: In a non-threatening tone of voice, Mr. Smith says, *"Thank you, Mrs. James, for coming to this meeting. As the guidance counselor, one of my jobs is to be available to talk with the students when things are troubling them. At times,* *students are referred to me by their teachers because of something that happened in the classroom. Twice, Jeremy has been sent to see me by his P. E. teacher because of his teasing other students and hitting them. On both of those occasions, Jeremy said that he was sorry and agreed to stop the behavior. Following the last visit, which was two weeks ago, Jeremy has since been referred to the principal for the same behavior. I've looked at Jeremy's cumulative folder, which includes records that date back to kindergarten."* At this point he hands Mrs. James a report card, attendance printout and discipline file. After giving Mrs. James a few minutes to look over the material, he continues, *"In looking at his test scores and grades, it's clear that Jeremy is bright and capable. It wasn't until last year in third grade that we noticed a slight drop in grades and an increase in discipline referrals. This did not happen until the last six-week period. In looking at his discipline file, you can see that this year Jeremy has been referred to the principal on three occasions, and each time he has received a consequence. My concern is that in spite of the consequences, Jeremy seems unable to stop his behavior. We don't like giving consequences when we don't think they are working."* Continuing to refer to the data, *"You can see by his attendance record that he has six excused absences this year, with five of them on Mondays."*

**Mom:** In a defensive posture she explains, *"Well, he's been ill a lot lately. In addition, there are times he sleeps so heavily that I can't wake him up, so I figure he needs his rest."*

**Counselor:** Without making judgments or asking questions, the counselor continues to refer to the data and says, *"Currently his grades are as follows: Math-55, Science-70, Language Arts-63, P.E.-75, Music-80, and Art-95. My concern is that when I look at all these things: grades, attendance, discipline referrals and my visits with Jeremy; it leads me to believe there is something interfering with his ability to learn that apparently was not a factor until last year."*

**Mom:** Reacting strongly, standing up, and stepping back from the table, she challenges, *"Are you saying he's brain damaged or something? Because, if you are, then you'd better back those words up with a medical degree. Or are you saying that he's stupid?"*

**Principal:** Remaining seated, with no reaction to the anger, she reassures her, *"Neither, Mrs. James. What we are saying is that Jeremy's behavior has been inappropriate and that our attempts to redirect him have not worked. I believe* *that if Jeremy could redirect his own behavior; he would. No one likes to get in trouble. But at this time, he doesn't seem to be able to change his behavior. His teacher has a tallied up sheet that includes observations and concerns from all of Jeremy's teachers. We have a copy of this for you and we will give it to you at the end of this meeting."*

**Mom**: *"Good, I'd like to know what they are seeing. It couldn't be nearly as bad as you two have expressed!"* She sits and squarely faces Jeremy's teacher and says: *"Tell me what he's like in your classroom, Ms. Loveless."*

**Teacher**: In an open and straightforward manner, she says, *"Mrs. James, I will be very happy to tell you exactly what I'm seeing in the classroom. In addition, I will share information from Jeremy's other teachers. We don't know what is going on, but we do know that if we don't come up with something that works, Jeremy is going to continue to experience negative consequences, and that isn't fair to him. Mrs. James, I'm going to read from a sheet that I've copied for you. Before I start, I want you to know that I like Jeremy, as do his other teachers. He's bright, and at times he's a pleasure to teach. He has a wonderful sense of humor, knows how to ask for help when he needs it and seems sensitive towards others. This is why we are concerned about Jeremy. Unfortunately, we see some patterns of behavior that seem to have increased lately. A total of six teachers work with Jeremy every day. His Math, Science, Language Arts, Music, Art, and his PE teachers have all provided information for this meeting. Before I start with the sheet, are there any questions?"*

**Mom**: Taking a different tack, she asks, *"Is this stuff going to go in his permanent records? I mean, the way our schools are . . . . this stuff will follow him around all his life."*

**Principal**: Speaking softly, yet with authority, she says, *"None of this goes in Jeremy's permanent file. It will be locked in Mr. Smith's office and destroyed at the end of the year. You are welcome to see this information anytime you want, and a copy will be given to you today."*

**Teacher**: Taking her time, she begins highlighting the tallied-up behavior observation sheet. *"The numbers you see on the sheet indicate the number of Jeremy's teachers who have observed the patterns of behavior in their classes. It seems that we are focusing on the negative, but please be assured that we recognize Jeremy's strengths and will do whatever it takes to help him succeed.*

*Regarding academic performance, of the six teachers who work with Jeremy, five have observed declining grades, two are concerned about academic failure, and three see inconsistent daily work. All six of his teachers see excessive absenteeism and three have seen a pattern of missing school on Monday."* Ms. Loveless pauses to give Mrs. James time to absorb the information, and then continues, *"Regarding conduct, five teachers have observed Jeremy being impulsive, excessively demanding, and demonstrating erratic behavior changes. He doesn't display this in Art, which he currently has a ninety-five. Five are concerned about inattentiveness and his being easily distracted and fidgety. It seems he does not care as much as he used to."*

**Mom:** In disbelief, she explodes, *"I can't understand what I'm hearing. If things are this serious, why haven't we met before? You make it sound like he's the worst thing in the world. I'll admit he's a handful, but he's not completely rotten."*

**Principal:** *"We don't think he's rotten at all. When we started adding all these things together, we realized that Jeremy needs some help. I'm sorry that we have not met before but I am glad we are meeting today. We've tried several things here on campus, with little success. What we need to do is take it one step further."*

**Mom:** Again standing, grabbing her purse, she challenges, *"What do you mean . . . take it further? You aren't going to expel him are you?"*

**Principal:** In a reassuring voice, she says, *"No. We want him to stay here and succeed as a student, and the best way we know for him to do that is to give you a recommendation that we think will help. Before I give that recommendation, are there any questions or comments?"*

**Mom:** She sits with a look of distrust on her face. *"Is this recommendation going to cost me money? Because if it is, then you can forget it."*

**Principal:** *"First of all, Mrs. James, it does not cost you anything. What we all agree on is that Jeremy could benefit from what we call a behavioral health assessment. This assessment can be done here at school or off campus, based on your preference, and it is facilitated by someone who doesn't work for the school system. I have a list of four people in our community who are able and* *willing to provide free assessments to students and parents. Are you familiar with community based assessments?*

**Mom**: Still frowning, she responds, *"Sort of. It's some meeting to find out if Jeremy is crazy or if I'm a bad mother, right?"*

**Counselor**: Quickly responding to Mrs. James, she says, *"I can tell you this, the assessment is not going to determine if you are a good or bad parent, or even surmise that Jeremy is "crazy". Actually, the best description is that an assessment is an interview between you, Jeremy, and a skilled assessor. The assessor will ask questions that pertain to school and home. I hope that the assessment will reveal what is going on with Jeremy, so that we can help him more effectively. Many of our students have gone through this process, and we are very pleased with how things have turned out. The assessor will make recommendations to you that you are not obligated to follow, though we hope that you do. Are there any questions about this assessment?"*

**Mom**: With a little less defiance, she tests, *"Yeah! What if I don't want to do it? Are you going to kick my kid out of your school?"*

**Principal**: Responding to the test, she answers, *"You have every right to say no to this assessment, but understand we have a right to have students act appropriately and be teachable. This assessment is our best attempt to see this happen. If you choose not to do it, then we, as a school, are forced to continue doing the same things, such as discipline referrals and visits to Mr. Smith. So far these things haven't worked, and we don't think they will now. Do you understand what I'm saying?"*

**Mom**: Showing a bit more interest, she exclaims, *"I guess so! What if Jeremy doesn't want to do it?"*

**Counselor**: Showing support for Mrs. James, she offers, *"We aren't concerned with that as much as we are pleased to see you considering the assessment. If you would like, we can go into my office and make some phone calls. Would you rather do the assessment here, at school or off campus?"*

**Mom:** Still tentative, she says, *"Here would be easier, but what do I tell Jeremy?"*

**Counselor**: *"If you want, I will be happy to inform him about the recommendations we have agreed upon.*

**Mom**: Responding in a more relaxed tone, *"I'd appreciate that. This meeting wasn't as bad as I expected. I thought you were going to tell me Jeremy was bad and that I had better do something about it. To tell you the truth, I've been worried for a long time about him. Maybe this will help."*

**Teacher**: Standing, she states, *"I also want to thank you for coming in today. Already, I have more positive feelings about what will happen with Jeremy. When I inform his other teachers that we met with you and things went well, I'm sure they'll feel the same way. Anytime you want to talk about how he's doing in class, please call me. In about a week, Mr. Smith will call to see how things are and see if we can do anything."*

**Principal**: In a positive tone of voice says, *"I wish all of the parents that we have met with were as helpful as you have been. My feeling is that with all of us working in the same direction for Jeremy, the chances of success are great. It is important that you complete this assessment so we can move forward. The assessor will request your permission to talk with us, so please consider this. Meanwhile, consider us an open door policy; anytime you have questions or need us to do something, please call."*

## Remember

√ Plan for this meeting. Go over with the other team members what will be said and what the goal of the meeting is. Get a consensus among each other prior to meeting with the parents; any appearance of uncertainty or disagreement is toxic to the outcome.

√ Do not overwhelm parents with a large number of participants. The intent is to collaborate and create a supportive environment for all.

√ All participants should have an assigned role in the meeting. This is to avoid anyone appearing to be an "observer". Parents don't need observers; they need supporters. Knowing ahead of time what each others' role is contributes a great deal to the success of this meeting.

What makes this particular meeting format work? The potential for a blow up was high as was the amount of negative information shared. The approach was collaborative rather than oppositional. Positive comments about Jeremy were made prior to any attempt at discussing concerns. Words such as "bad" or "problem" were not used and the team did not engage in any school-related acronyms. Mom was neither put on the defensive, nor talked down to.

Detachment and objectivity were maintained by all participating team members. Mom was given the chance to vent and ask questions without interruption. When concerns were shared, they were done specifically rather than generally. Blanket statements were avoided and information was shared in a matter of fact manner. Jeremy's best interests were kept a priority.

*Perseverance Furthers*
*I Ching*

# Chapter 19

# Meet the Parents

There are several reasons parents come to school for meetings ranging from *Back to School* night to student suspensions. In cases when the purpose of the meeting is to make suggestions or brainstorm ideas, a specific format is very helpful. Structured meetings end on time and almost always accomplish the established goals. In my experience, working with student assistance teams, the percentage of parents who responded well to any suggestions the team made exceeded eighty percent.

## A Backhanded Compliment

I have done about four hundred behavioral health assessments for middle and high school students, always with parent involvement. Out of curiosity, I would ask the parents each time how they felt about the meeting at school that suggested this assessment. I really anticipated hearing some anger, bitterness, resentment and irritation. Typically the responses were things like; *"My husband and I didn't know what to do. We are so grateful the school was able to help."* Another comment made more than once was, *"I didn't know the school cared this much; I really appreciate the school's help."* Some variations of these comments were what I almost always heard. The one time I heard differently was noteworthy. Mrs. Luna was a single mother of a seventh grade student who had failed the seventh grade the prior year. His behavior had shifted considerably from how he was in sixth grade. The problems Joseph displayed last year were such that Mrs. Luna made an appointment to speak with his counselor. She was seeking some help she claimed did not get any answers.

Mrs. Luna responded to my question about the meeting she had at school this year in this manner; *"That damn school. Last year when Joseph was failing the seventh grade, I called his counselor and met with her; she didn't help. Now Joseph is starting to fail the seventh grade again and I get a phone call inviting me to a meeting. At this meeting, people had ideas and suggestions that could help".* She paused for a second and continued; *"Why didn't they do this team meeting last year?"* Her comment was a backhanded compliment of the SAP meeting. The previous year, the school did not have the SAP and this year they do; this year Mrs. Luna was helped. Last year she felt abandoned. Following the behavioral health assessment, Joseph entered residential treatment for chemical dependency. This happened many years ago and I often wonder what kind of an adult Joseph became. The last time I saw him was in court. His father was suing mom for custody of the kids. I was asked to serve as a witness verifying that Mr. Luna had been abusive with Joseph. This was an issue that he worked on while in my group, and I felt comfortable discussing the accusation. When the opposing lawyer asked me how I could have remembered Joseph out of all the hundreds of teenagers I've worked with, I told him that Joseph was the only kid who had ever urinated on the nurse's station wall. Our side won the ruling.

Studies have shown that on average, parents wait up to two years after first realizing there is a problem before taking a firm stand. It takes time to get past rationalizations such as: "It's just a phase, boys will be boys, and I did the same when I was her age and countless others." A good intervention helps parents shorten the period of time between the first realization that there is a problem and taking action.

*"Honest good humor is the oil and wine of a merry meeting and there is no jovial companionship equal to that where the jokes are rather small and laughter abundant."*
**Washington Irving**

## Parent Meeting Agenda

The purpose of meeting a student's parents may vary, but there are some basic considerations that if followed, can help ensure the time is well spent. These considerations should not get in the way of your personal style that is uniquely yours and can be a huge benefit to the outcome of the meeting. Inversely, style can be a huge impediment to the success of the intervention. Assuming that this meeting is a face-to-face event (as opposed to telephone), there are physical concerns worth examining.

## Seating Arrangements

Avoid setting up the room so that there is an "us against them" sentiment concerning the seating arrangements. Sitting behind a desk is not a good idea. It sets up a barrier from the beginning that can only get in the way. Sitting around a table can be a good way to set up a meeting. If not around a table, then place the chairs in a format that fosters an open environment. It is even helpful to avoid sitting in a chair that is bigger or sits higher than the other chairs in the room. This meeting is not meant to establish hierarchy; it is to work with parents in a collaborative fashion.

**Teacher with Parent(s)**

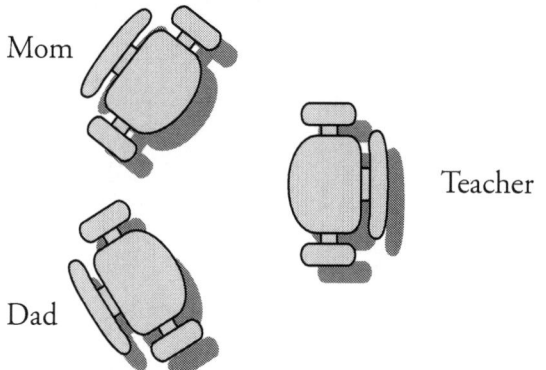

Mom

Teacher

Dad

**Team with Parent(s)**

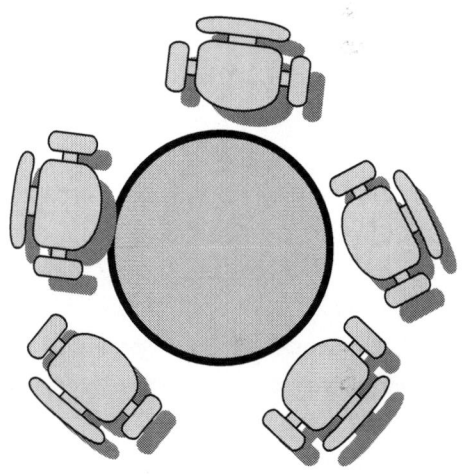

If a team is scheduled to meet with a parent or parents, be aware that a parent entering a room with a number of people sitting around a table can be extremely intimidating. Be empathetic; how you might feel in the same situation? A suggestion that works is for all team members to meet the parents at the door and give the parents the first choice of where they want to sit. When the parents are seated, then the team chooses seats. A meeting should not start until all parties are there. Interruptions by late arrivers only serve to knock the agenda off course.

*"Good fortune is what happens when opportunity meets with planning."*
**Thomas Edison**

## Outline of a Parent Meeting Agenda

1) **Introductions**—everyone is introduced and has a clear role—no observers.
2) **Establish purpose**—ensure the objective of the meeting—clarify goal(s).
3) **Initial bonding**—comfortable conversation if possible—make parents feel welcome.
4) **Clarify parent's status**—invite questions, explain collaboration—reinforce parents' rights.
5) **Present specific concerns**—details are important, avoid generalizations—paint an accurate picture.
6) **Parent's response**—how specific concerns were received-move beyond any parental denial.
7) **Venting and questioning**—parent's time to express feelings, etc.—they should feel heard.
8) **Establishing strategies**—brainstorm possible options with parents—look at all available options.
9) **Determine specific strategies**—consensus reached by all, prioritize plan and establish follow up date.
10) **Wrap up**—positive invitation to keep communication open and to continue contacting the school.
11) **Process meeting**—after parents leave, discuss the process and how well it worked.

*"Diplomacy is to do and say the nastiest things in the nicest way."*
**Isaac Goldberg**

## Heads up about the Meeting

Explain the purpose of the meeting. Don't assume the parents know why the meeting is being held. As a parent it is easy to "make up" the reason and assume a negative spin. Defensiveness is fairly ordinary and has very little to do with you. There are times that this isn't true and the entire focus is on how a teacher has treated a student. It is estimated that ten percent of teachers can be considered bullies. A parent may well request a meeting to clarify some things that are happening in a classroom. In that case, it may have a lot do with you. I suspect anyone who would take the time to read this book is not a bully; sorry, if I am preaching to the choir.

If possible, review the purpose of the meeting which is to ensure that everyone is on a similar page and working together for the benefit of the student. Side note: *The team should have met beforehand to reach a consensus on what suggestions or recommendations need to be made for the student at the intervention meeting.* This collaborative approach may at first be questionable to the parents, but eventually mom or dad will see that it is legitimate. If appropriate, stress the confidentiality of the meeting and that it will focus on school-related issues, such as grades, attendance and classroom behavior. Let the parents know that copies of all the information covered can be provided to them at the end of the meeting, including documents that apply to the primary concern of the meeting such as progress reports, attendance records, etc. Encourage the parents to ask questions and provide whatever input they feel is important.

Remember that most parents will be feeling intimidated, nervous, guilty, angry, afraid, or inadequate at the beginning of this meeting. Again, be sensitive to what it is like to come to the school to discuss concerns regarding a child. Chances are the parents have been to the school before and may have had a negative experience, leaving them with the proverbial "chip on the shoulder". You may be on the receiving end of their frustrations so remain detached and supportive.

Hopefully, the "nastiest" things are not intended to be said, but the point of the above quote is made. Always start with reporting the student's strengths while maintaining a tone of voice that is matter-of-fact. Avoid talking down or using school-related acronyms. Make eye contact and speak to both parents (if both are attending). Often the mistake is made by speaking to the more verbal parent, neglecting the parent who is more reserved or quiet. Once the strengths are shared, present the rest of your concerns and observations. Stay as focused on school as possible. Unless the parents bring up the home environment, be careful to not step on any emotional landmines.

In a parent meeting, asking questions is a part of the process. How these questions are asked determines whether or not they help. Parents can and do read between the lines. Veiled accusations wrapped in a question are intrusive and offensive.

When sharing these observations, there is a fine line between overwhelming the parents with too many details and skimming so shallow that an inaccurate picture is painted. Interruptions by the parents are normal and should be dealt with in a patient manner. Take the time to answer all questions as completely as you can. Even when challenged by a parent, avoid becoming defensive or blaming. One of the primary objectives of this meeting is to create an alliance with the parents.

As the meeting begins to wrap up, make sure the parent leaves without any unspoken concerns. Tell them that if something comes up that they feel needs to be shared, that they should give you a call; you want to keep the line of communication open. Double-check phone numbers and ask the parent if there is anything special he or she wants or needs from you. Put the parent in the driver's seat regarding the student's education. *On the continuum of teacher personalities the gamut runs from humble to arrogant. Ego usually gets in the way of collaboration with others. A strong ego is not high self-esteem; it is a defensive posture of self-aggrandizement to ward off what is lurking below the surface which is usually self-doubt.*

How this meeting is approached can set the tone for months to come. For the short time that parents are sitting down with you, it would pay dividends to treat this time as the most important task at hand; for them it often is. Many of the teachers I've worked with have had questionable experiences as parents of their own children. Maybe you know exactly what it is like to walk into a room feeling anxious, scared, and frustrated. If not, consider yourself fortunate. Parents need encouragement, support and understanding as much as students, sometimes more.

## Words poorly Chosen

A well-meaning teacher once attempted to assure the parents of a struggling boy that all was not lost and that the school year could still end on a good note. Unfortunately, her choice of words ended up creating more turmoil.

Below is her statement. A more appropriate statement to say the same thing follows:

Her well intended comment:
*"I'm sure your son is salvageable."*

What the teacher could have said:
*"There are all kinds of things we can do to make this a positive year."*

## Be Careful with Questions

Is there a history of mental health problems in your family tree?
Where did you learn that parenting technique?
Did you screw up when you were a child?
Does your husband drink too much?
What kind of prescription drugs does your wife take?
Why didn't you seek help sooner for your child?

There can be no greater of an ally than a student's parents. However, the opposite can be stated also. Some parents support the school and teacher; others seem to blame the school and teacher for every problem displayed by their child. Regardless, it is imperative to communicate and work with parents when needed. When meeting face-to-face, the setting and structure are important. Planning the meeting, with a clear agenda, keeps the meeting on task. The skills used in the meeting are key to its success. This chapter can be a great resource. Consider reading it before your next parent meeting, if needed.

One issue that is so important that it deserves its own chapter is confidentiality. Ethically, honoring the trust of someone cannot be argued. Legally, there are established norms for you to follow. Be aware that some of those norms contradict others.

*"If you forfeit the confidence of your fellow citizens, you can never get it back."*
**Abraham Lincoln**

# Chapter 20

# Confidentiality

I can think of little else that can be as aggravating as when confidentiality is used as a power play by an individual. It is the kid on the playground chanting; "I know something that you don't know." There are legitimate times when those who work with students need to share information when it is in the student's best interest. Most of us who work with kids have strong ethics. Yet, there are times when what is known about a student is no one's business. It doesn't help the student and some people love to gossip. For those professional therapists and counselors, the standards of confidentiality are clear and supported by law. We all have a right to privacy. Once again, the Golden Rule applies; Do unto others what you want done to you.

Parents have a right to know about their child's grades, attendance, and classroom behavior. On the other hand, information the counselor or nurse possesses often needs to be kept confidential. This is information disclosed by the student in private that is not necessarily school-related. Examples of the information that should remain confidential include a student's disclosure of pregnancy, drug use, relationship issues, etc. A good rule of thumb is to avoid sharing too much information with other faculty members unless there is a legitimate reason. Teacher lounge or break-room gossip exists in schools, businesses and any other places people gather. Minimizing this by not contributing to the gossip is a good policy.

Parent meetings may be the "window of opportunity" for the teacher and parents to strengthen a collaborative relationship. The ability to communicate directly can be the seed in which the tree of understanding flourishes. There is a fine balance between what is discussed and what is confidential. Kids do have rights to have certain information kept confidential from others, even parents and guardians. Each state determines the age in which a child has the right to confidentiality. Know your local laws concerning this issue.

## What Do You Think?

Below, are examples of different statements that require some decision on whether or not any are appropriate. Most of these are blatant violations of confidentiality and one is appropriate. When in doubt, act in the student's best interest.

"Mrs. Smith, I am not supposed to tell you, but your daughter is pregnant. Do you want the number to an agency that can take care of it?"

"Mr. Jones, your son told me that he has smoked pot before. You need to set some boundaries."

"Charles, your mother and father called me and told me they are getting a divorce. They said you didn't know about it, but I think it is best you know."

"Sara, your mother called and asked me to find out if you are still a virgin. I told her I'd see what I could find out."

"Jennifer, what kind of rumors do you hear regarding Sharon? I need to know what the students are saying."

"Mr. and Mrs. Ramez, I am calling to let you know your son has been engaging in bullying behavior in my class and isn't responding to me. Has this happened before?"

*"I'm not sure what is more painful, the bullying itself or the blatant indifference of those around."*
**Donna Clark Love**

# Chapter 21

# Bullying Behaviors in Class

Bullies lurk at every grade level in school. They are known to go "shopping for their victims". Bullying occurs in hallways, in cafeterias, on buses, on playgrounds, and while walking home. And of course, bullying abounds in the classroom. When you see it, how do you respond? A book on intervention has to include information designed to help classroom teachers and other educators know specific steps to take when bullying is observed.

When someone possessing more power than another and repeatedly intimidates, hits, haunts, victimizes, humiliates, degrades and shames another . . . it is called bullying. Bullying occurs in all grades by both boys and girls. For boys, bullying acts tend to be more physical. For girls, bullying acts tend to be more focused on damaging relationships. Adults bully other adults and approximately ten percent of teachers bully students (my ninth grade teacher Ms. Bane).

It is vital to have an established policy on bullying for every classroom. This should include how it will be confronted and what will occur if it continues. Below are suggested guidelines for teachers who are seeking to put an end to what is quickly becoming a crisis, not just in frequency but in degree of harm.

The information listed below was provided as a courtesy of my wife, Donna Clark Love, who is a nationally known consultant and trainer for schools seeking to address bullying and other issues.

## Preventing Bullying
### Good ideas that apply to the classroom

★ Let students know bullying will not be tolerated.
★ Post rules and consequences and consistently reinforce.
★ Teach respect & empathy for all.
★ Offer students ways to report bullying.
★ Listen to what is not said; read between the lines.
★ Encourage students to get involved in school activities.
★ Model behavior you expect from your students.
★ Control your emotions: If the student who bullies knows you get easily angered, you can become the target of masterful "button pushing".
★ Learn the beginning signs of "acting out behaviors" of potential bullies so you can intervene before a "meltdown" occurs and "nip it in the bud."
★ Build a relationship with students.
★ Offer encouragement and support to students who have been victimized.

## Intervening with Bully Behavior

**When bullying is observed in the classroom, the teacher should do the following:**

√ Immediately tell the bully to "Stop"!
√ Stand between the student who bullies and the one who is bullied . . . blocking eye contact.
√ Escort the victim to another area.
√ Support the bullied student by asking to talk later.
√ Write a note describing the incident & turn it in to the office.

## When Talking with the Target

√  Be calm
√  Be supportive and accept feelings
√  Actively listen
√  Help child find solutions

## Teaching Self-Protection

√  Model assertiveness—it can be learned.
   o  Assertiveness is telling someone exactly what you want (directly
      and respectively).
   o  We confuse being assertive with being aggressive.
√  Teach child to "act" un-phased when confronted.
√  Assertiveness leads to healthy self-esteem.
√  There is often a strong urge to tell the victim to fight back. Don't! You
   can tell the child that he or she has a right to take up for him or herself.
   The power differential is such that by urging a child to fight a bully
   pushes him or her into a scary and sometimes dangerous situation.

Make your classroom a safe harbor. Let students know that if they need a
place to get away, your classroom is available.

## Possible Discipline Consequences for the Bully

Below are some suggestions for the classroom regarding discipline consequences for students who bully. When an adult ignores the behavior, the victim is abandoned and the bystander remains apathetic.

1. Warning
2. Meeting w/counselor / send letter home to parents or make a phone call
3. In house suspension/ restricted safety plan/ loss of school freedoms
4. Intervention w/parents (student present), documentation presented, consequences determined by school w/parent input, if appropriate

## Twelve Steps to Stop Bullying

| | |
|---|---|
| 1. Immediately stop the bullying. | 7. Talk separately with the bully and victim. |
| 2. Conspicuously support the victim. | 8. Begin with the victim, then the bully. |
| 3. Name the bullying behavior. | 9. Impose sanctions to the bully. |
| 4. Refer to the school rules. | 10. Report the incident to colleagues. |
| 5. Impose immediate consequences. | 11. Talk with the parents. |
| 6. Empower the bystanders. | 12. Follow-up later. |

*"What we do not see, what most of us never suspect of existing, is the silent but irresistible power which comes to the rescue of those who fight on in the face of discouragement."*
***Napoleon Hill***

## Talking After the Bullying

√   Be calm

√   Ask the student if he/she wants help

√   Listen carefully. Ask questions to clarify the details.

- Who was involved?
- What happened?
- When?
- Where?
- Were there any witnesses?

√   Be patient; don't expect all of the details to come pouring out. The student may be reluctant to give details.

√   Avoid questions that imply he or she might have done something wrong or "deserved" the bullying.

√   If the student skirts the issue, let him/her know that you are willing to talk when he/she is ready.

√   Redouble your efforts to create a positive classroom where bullying is not tolerated.

√   Let the student know you believe what he/she is telling you.

√   Ask the student if he/she has any ideas for changing the situation.

√   Offer specific suggestions. If you are not sure what to say, let the student know you will get back with him/her.

√   If at any time a student mentions, threatens, or alludes to suicide, get help.

## Help, Teacher Help?

Sadly, some adults are non responsive when a student within eyesight is being bullied. When questioned, students suggest that about eighty percent of the teachers who observe bullying don't do anything. When teachers are given the same questionnaire, seventy-five percent claim they step in and deal with it. What a huge disparity between what students and teachers think. Some of the rationalizations used by adults on why they ignore or turn their backs when bullying is occurring:

*Boys will be boys!*
*It's none of my business.*
*Well, maybe he deserves it.*
*It will toughen him or her up.*
*Oh, you know how girls can be.*
*It's really not as bad as it looks.*
*It is a normal part of childhood.*
*She kind of brought it on herself.*
*I was bullied and I turned out all right.*
*Someone else will take care of it—I'm sure of it!*
*He'll do something about the bullying when he's sick and tired of it.*

Bullying hurts and can inflict damage that is felt for years. Bullying can be stopped; it just takes someone to step up. You may be the only one who does.

For in-depth information and state-of-art training on this subject, contact

**Donna Clark Love**
*donna@clark-love.com*

Office Phone Number
(281) 467-4861

*"When you have an elephant by the leg and it's trying to run away;*
*it's best to let him run."*
**Abraham Lincoln**

# Chapter 22

# Detachment

Detachment is the ability to remain involved and dedicated without losing sight of what can and cannot be controlled. Being detached is a way of avoiding the emotional roller-coaster ride along with the person you are concerned about. Detachment is the ability to remember you did not cause the pain; you cannot cure it, but you can cope. Carrying someone else's feelings is a burden few can endure very long. To do so consistently is a form of co-dependency. It is so important to know the difference between your feelings and the feelings of others'. Blurring these lines is an indicator of your own boundaries being fuzzy.

We only have control of what we do, not over what other people do. When intervening, we do have control over what we say, how we say it and our attitude. But, the outcome is not in our hands. Doing the best you can and letting go of the results is one of the most valuable lessons one can learn when intervening. Ultimately no intervention really fails when the big picture is considered. At the very least, a seed is planted. It may take more tragedy to fertilize and water the seedling. Crisis and trauma may end up serving as the sunlight needed for fruition to occur.

*"Ward, I'm worried about the Beaver.*
**June Cleaver, Mayfield circa 1959**

June Cleaver was a model for how to not let go. She worried, fretted and sought consolation from Ward anytime Wally and the Beave were either out of the house, or being too quiet upstairs in their bedroom. Contrary to her hand wringing, it is suggested that letting go is healthier and easier. To not let go, is to worry. To worry is to waste emotional energy. For we all know that no one ever changed a thing by worrying. For example, I can worry about having a flat tire, and it will not change the fact that I either will or will not. Has anyone ever added an inch to their height by worrying?

## Letting Go

Letting go is not to deny, but to accept.

Letting go is to fear less, and love more.

Letting go is not to fix, but to be supportive.

Letting go is not to care for, but to care about.

Letting go is not to be protective; it is to permit another to face reality.

Letting go is not to regret the past, but to grow and live for now and the future.

Letting go is not to criticize and regulate others, but to be the best can you be.

Letting go is not to be in the middle arranging, but to be on the sidelines cheering.

Letting go is not enabling others; it is to allow others to learn from natural consequences.

Letting go is to not stop caring; it is not to take responsibility for someone else.

Letting go is not to blame others, but to make the most of yourself and the situation.

Letting go is not to cut yourself off from others, it is realizing you can't control others.

Letting go is to admit your own powerlessness; the outcome is not in your hands.

Letting go is not to nag, scold, argue; it is to search out and correct your own shortcomings.

# The Dangers of Labeling

For the most part, labeling serves the labeler rather than the labeled. When one labels another, he/she places people in categories that best describes their behaviors or symptoms. Labeling tends to stem from the pathology model of looking for what is wrong. Usually a label carries a negative association, begging for the student to live up (or down) to the expectations which may become a self-fulfilling prophecy planted by adults.

*"He's the **black sheep** of the family."*
*"That boy is just one **big baby.**"*
*"I don't know what she sees in him; **he's a loser.**"*
*"Our low performing students are our **flat liners**."*
*"You know, she's an **at risk student**."*

*"To get through the hardest journey we need to take only one step at a time, but we must keep on stepping."*
**Chinese Proverb**

# Chapter 23

# Self Care

Being overwhelmed or desensitized are good reasons an individual needs to take care of the *mental, physical, spiritual and social* aspects that make up a whole person. Neglect of any of these areas seems to diminish our ability to weather the storms or traumas routinely whirling our way. There are so many ways people take care of themselves that there will be no attempt to capture all in this section. Just a few of these include: *eating healthy, exercising, enjoying a hobby, creating an immediate circle of friends for support, working with a mentor, attending 12-step meetings, seeing a skilled therapist, or simply taking a vacation (man, this last one really sounds good).* When the burden of someone else's trauma gets too large to endure, the experience of thousands has shown that 12-step meetings provide relief. A person needs to be able to detach and let go of situations beyond control. This is a primary intent of meetings such as Adult Children of Alcoholics, Alanon, and Emotions Anonymous. If the co-dependent pain eventually gets too intense, it is comforting to know these solutions are available. It seems though that we often wait until the pain becomes unbearable before reaching out for help. But, who takes care of the caretaker?

## Two Marbles in the Pocket

I carry two marbles in my pockets as I walk through each day
There are two front pockets; one left and one right
The marbles are not fancy or rare; just regular old marbles
It is not their size or their color that I value
It is what they represent
They represent something of importance to me
My place in the big picture of life
Who am I?
Why am I here?
How do I fit in?
How important am I?
Are other people just as important?
One marble stands for the belief that for my sake, the universe was created
God's entire glorious creation
The planets and even galaxies of stars
The other marble reminds me of another perspective
I am one single grain of sand on a long sandy beach
I am no more or no less
I am but one of the many
When reaching for a marble
The key is to know what pocket to choose

## How do you Sharpen your Saw?

Working with children, whether in elementary or secondary school, is often taxing. Even when appropriately and effectively detached, we pour part of ourselves into the work we do with students. We run dry, and often lose that spark that ignites the students' desire to learn. How do we get it back? How do you replenish the vitality central to your own wellbeing?

In Stephen Covey's, *Seven Habits for Highly Effective People*, he lists sharpening the saw as the seventh habit touted in his popular book. He uses the term "self-renewal" as a reference to maintaining balanced wellbeing.

## Ten Self-Care Techniques

*This brochure was shared at http://www.ucc.vt.edu/stdysk/stresmgt.html by Virginia Polytechnic Institute and State University*

1. TO RELAX. Throughout the day, take "mini-breaks". Sit down and get comfortable. Slowly take in a deep breath; hold it; and then exhale very slowly. At the same time, let your shoulder muscles droop, smile, and say something positive like, "I am r-e-l-a-x-e-d." Be sure to get sufficient rest at night.
2. PRACTICE ACCEPTANCE. Many people get distressed over things they won't let themselves accept. Often, these are things that can't be changed, for example someone else's feelings or beliefs. If something unjust bothers you, that is different. If you act in a responsible way, the chances are you will manage that stress effectively.
3. TALK RATIONALLY TO YOURSELF. Ask yourself what real impact the stressful situation will have on you in a day or in a week, and see if you can let the negative thoughts go. Think through whether the situation is your problem or the other person's. If it is yours, approach it calmly and firmly. If it is the other person's, there is not much you can do about it. Rather than condemning yourself with hindsight thinking like, "I should have . . . ," think about what you can learn from the error and plan for the future. Watch out for perfectionism—set realistic and attainable goals. Remember: everyone makes errors. Be careful of procrastination—practice

breaking tasks into smaller units to make it manageable, and practice prioritizing to get things done.

4.  GET ORGANIZED. Develop a realistic schedule of daily activities that includes time for work, sleep, relationships, and recreation. Use a daily "thing to do" list. Improve your physical surroundings by cleaning your classroom, house and your office. Use your time and energy efficiently.

5.  EXERCISE. Physical activity has always provided relief from stress. In the past, daily work was largely physical. Now that physical exertion is no longer a requirement for earning a living, we don't get rid of stress so easily. It accumulates very quickly. We need to develop a regular exercise program to reduce the effects of stress before it becomes distress. Try aerobics, walking, jogging, dancing, or swimming.

6.  REDUCE TIME URGENCY. If you frequently check your watch or worry about what you do with your time, learn to take things a bit slower. Allow plenty of time to get things done. Plan your schedule ahead of time. Recognize that you can only do so much in a given period. Practice the notion of "pace, not race".

7.  QUIET TIME. Balance your family, social, and work demands with special private times. Hobbies are good antidotes for daily pressures. Unwind by taking a quiet stroll, soaking in a hot bath, watching a sunset, or listening to calming music.

8.  WATCH YOUR HABITS. Eat sensibly—a balanced diet will provide all the necessary energy you will need during the day. Minimize the use nonprescription drugs and alcohol—you need to be mentally and physically alert to deal with stress. Be mindful of the effects of excessive caffeine and sugar on nervousness. Put out the cigarettes—they restrict blood circulation and affect the stress response.

9.  TALK TO FRIENDS. Friends can be good medicine. Daily doses of conversation, regular social engagements, and occasional sharing of deep feelings and thoughts can reduce stress quite nicely.

*Virginia Polytechnic Institute and State University*

So, what will you do? How will you take care of your physical, emotional, mental and spiritual self? On the next page, take a moment and list ways you will maintain a balance.

# A Window of Opportunity

| Physical | Emotional |
|---|---|
| 1. | 1. |
| 2. | 2. |
| 3. | 3. |
| 4. | 4. |
| 5. | 5. |
| **Mental** | **Spiritual** |
| 1. | 1. |
| 2. | 2. |
| 3. | 3. |
| 4. | 4. |
| 5. | 5. |

## Sanskrit Proverb

Look to this day,
For it is life,
The very life of life,
In its brief course lies all
The realities and verities of existence,
The bliss of growth,
The splendor of action,
The glory of power.
For yesterday is but a dream,
And tomorrow is only a vision.
But today well lived,
Makes every yesterday
A dream of happiness
And every tomorrow
A vision of hope.
Look well, therefore,
To this day.

*"Never give in . . . never, never, never, never, in nothing great or small, large or petty, never give in except to convictions of honour and good sense. Never yield to force . . . never yield to the apparently overwhelming might of the enemy."*
**Winston Churchill**

# Chapter 24

# When More is Needed

## The Student Assistance Program

Are there problems that students struggle with, yet, are beyond the school's capability or jurisdiction? When asked, teachers in my training sessions respond with a litany of familiar issues. These include *chemical dependency, divorce, serious mental illness, abuse, off campus violence, abject poverty, family destruction, poor nutrition, medical illness and suicide.* I then ask the rhetorical questions, "Do these serious problems interfere with student performance, attendance and behavior? Can a teacher effectively address these in class?" The point of these questions is to introduce the need for a school-based process that is effective in identifying and helping these students.

This process needs to not only identify these students, but also find a way to help parents engage community-based assistance that is equipped to address these issues. There needs to be a way to build a bridge between the school and community resources. Otherwise, students with issues beyond the school either depend on fate or fall through the crack. There have always been teachers who are able to contact the parents and successfully facilitate a connection with a community resource. However, this is not the rule, and most of these students are left to deal with things on their own. There needs to be a systemic process that does not rely on any one teacher. The eyes and ears that pick up on the indicators that a student has a serious problem belong to everyone on staff. Quite often, in retrospect, a comment will be made by a faculty member about recognizing evidence of a problem, but assumed it was an isolated incident, or there was no way to bring it to someone else's attention. This failure to notice or take action can be minimized when the right process is in place at school.

The framework that helps schools do just that is the Student Assistance Program (SAP). A study was done by the University of Pittsburg* contrasting two similar schools; one with the SAP and the other without. The school without the SAP was able to help about 20% of the students with behavioral health issues by making appropriate resources available. The school with the SAP was able to offer help to 80% of the students who needed it. It was not that one school had more problems than the other did one; it was one school that responded in a systemic way. Fewer students fell through the cracks.

## Four Basic Models

In the vast landscape (K-12, urban, rural, tiny and huge) that contains Student Assistance Programs, there are four general models for running the process. Within these general models are even more variations of the process. The choice on which model to use is often based on a school's available resources, personnel, and expectations. This chapter is written as a way to compare or contrast the different SAP models. Each is described below, with strengths and challenges listed. The complexity lies in the fact that a comprehensive and well-designed SAP is flexible in its responses, resisting any attempt to easily be placed within any one descriptive category. Expecting the SAP to stay within the parameters of model-driven cage is saying that there is only one path to take regardless of your destination. Forcing the process to adhere to arbitrarily drawn boundaries is rigid and uninspired. Never was the SAP intended as a bureaucratic process. On the contrary, SAPs should burn with a passion to give every student the chance to succeed, regardless of the model. After all, it's really the people that make the SAP work. Even the best process becomes rank and stale when devoid of passion and empathy.

The Four General SAP models include:

- ➤ Core Team model
- ➤ In-house Counselor model
- ➤ External SAP model
- ➤ Eclectic model

These models described, will include the strengths and challenges of each. The intent is to offer an objective look at what can often be a confusing kaleidoscope of terms, policies and procedures.

## Core Team Model

In this model, the campus has a team of about six to eight trained members to brain-storm appropriate interventions for identified students. This team meets regularly and often uses a case management system geared to ensure "nothing falls through the cracks". Decisions made by this team are usually based on observable, measurable school-related information such as grades, attendance and classroom behavior. *Core teams* work to develop strategies that include classroom interventions, referral to a campus-based support services, or possibly a suggestion to contact a community-based behavioral health facility for an assessment. The *core team* does not diagnose or provide direct services to the student. The team serves as an intervention and referral process, connecting students to the most appropriate resource available. It connects the dots.

The composition of the *core team* is a key to the SAP being broad-brushed, with the ability to serve a wide array of concerns. Often included is an administrator, guidance counselors, the nurse, a special education teacher, a couple of regular education teachers, school psychologist, attendance clerk, etc. A well conceived multi-disciplinary team can effectively respond to many types of problems students often struggle with at school, academic and behavioral.

The primary purpose of the *core team model* is to screen and connect students with the most appropriate resource available in the classroom, on campus, and/or in the community. In addition, the team brainstorms ways to impact the overall campus by promoting developmental assets, strengthening protective factors and reducing risk factors. The *core team* works closely with existing school efforts, such as strategies to reduce absenteeism, drug use or drop outs, often providing the link necessary to connect students and parents to resources that exist yet often are not utilized.

Strengths
> Does not require staffing budget—team consists of volunteers from faculty
> Strong buy-in at school level—it is owned by campus
> Broad-brushed in scope—team synergy
> Powerful screening/brain-storming tool (puts many heads together at once)

Challenges
> Hard to schedule meeting time when all members can attend
> Team members have other demanding responsibilities
> Turnover requires ongoing training to ensure team remains competent
> Hard to find a skillful interventionist to meet with parents

For a number of reasons a *core team model* seems to be the most popular. Almost all the schools I work with use some form of the *core team model*. Outside of *core team*, there are other effective ways schools implement SAP.

## In-house Counselor Model

With this model, schools dedicate one or more staff positions to carry out SAP services. Usually this person has a clinical or counseling background. Referrals are made directly to this SAP counselor, who then determines the best course of action. This course may include the student continuing to see the counselor, participation in a campus-based support group or a referral to a community resource. This SAP model provides more direct services and is more clinical in nature. SAP counselors in this model tend to carry a caseload, working directly with students.

The primary purpose of the *internal counselor model* is to provide direct services to students who have been identified. This person serves as a counselor, an interventionist and a case manager for each student referred to the SAP, working with those referred students who are appropriate and referring elsewhere when more help is needed.

Strengths
> Scheduling much easier without a team
> Highly skilled SAP counselor has huge impact
> Does not require faculty members to volunteer to serve on a team

Challenges
> Requires budget for part or full time position
> SAP counselor often evolves (unintended) into school crisis counselor
> Tendency for counselor to try and handle most of the referrasl internally

This model has shown a strong impact when the SAP counselor is a good fit. A SAP counselor with sound clinical and intervention skills can really make a difference. On the other side of this coin is the reality that the wrong fit can seriously stifle the potential of the SAP at school.

## External SAP Model

This model relies upon a contractual relationship between a community agency and the school, where SAP services such as a individual counseling, support group facilitation and behavioral health assessments are provided. Generally, this model provides for ongoing direct services for students needing assistance.

The primary purpose of this model is to rely upon an outside agency to run the SAP. The details of the process are dictated by the schools, with the agency responsible for carrying out the mission. This mission may vary from school to school. An *external model* may utilize a core team process, or rely upon the single counselor format. In either case, the school contracts for these services.

Strengths
> Allows for a highly skilled clinician to assist students
> Scheduling is easier without a team

Challenges
> Requires budget
> Buy-in from school is a challenge
> Boundary confusion between school and agency

This model requires the community agency providing the contractual services to be very good at Student Assistance efforts. Many communities do not possess this resource, pushing the schools toward the core team or counselor model. In many cases, schools use parts of different models to form a more eclectic SAP.

## Eclectic or Hybrid Model

As a school's SAP evolves, it often changes; resulting in a core team process that uses SAP counselors. The core team provides the initial screening and intervention, with the counselors providing direct services such as support group or one-on-one counseling. In some schools, the SAP includes a team who serve as academic coaches, with others serving as mentors. The longer the SAP exists, the more prone it is to evolve into something even more comprehensive than the original process. A good suggestion is for the SAP to dedicate one meeting a month to planning this program evolution.

Strengths
> Built around school resources
> Often more comprehensive (broad-brushed)
> More resources available to connect students to

Challenges
> Budget needed to maintain program
> Often seen as soft, requiring strong tracking of success

## Some Things Are Universal

Underlying each of these SAP models are some basic parameters that ensure that the minimum standards are achieved. Allowing for the differences between models, can we still draw the line clear enough to spell out what needs to be in place in order to refer to the process as a SAP? The playing field is not level and students often need varying assistance.

Schools often have an early intervention team prior to SAP implementation. This team historically functioned to receive and screen students who were considered for Special or Exceptional Education services. It is difficult for faculty to shift this perception and utilize the existing early intervention team in a broad-brushed manner. Changing the name, or repackaging the process is helpful. Faculty needs to be reminded that the reason for a referral has broadened.

Staff meetings, in-services, flyers, posters and intentional verbal spreading of the message are great ways to remind the faculty of the change. The more transparent the referral process is, the better the buy-in by the faculty. Teachers need to know what happens following an initial referral.

There have been attempts to create an accurate and easy chart, and this one is my favorite. Donna Clark Love developed it during her tenure as administrator of a school district's Safe and Drug Free Schools and Communities department. Her permission to include it is appreciated. Below is a flowchart that captures the Student Assistance Program referral process very well.

# SAP Flow Chart

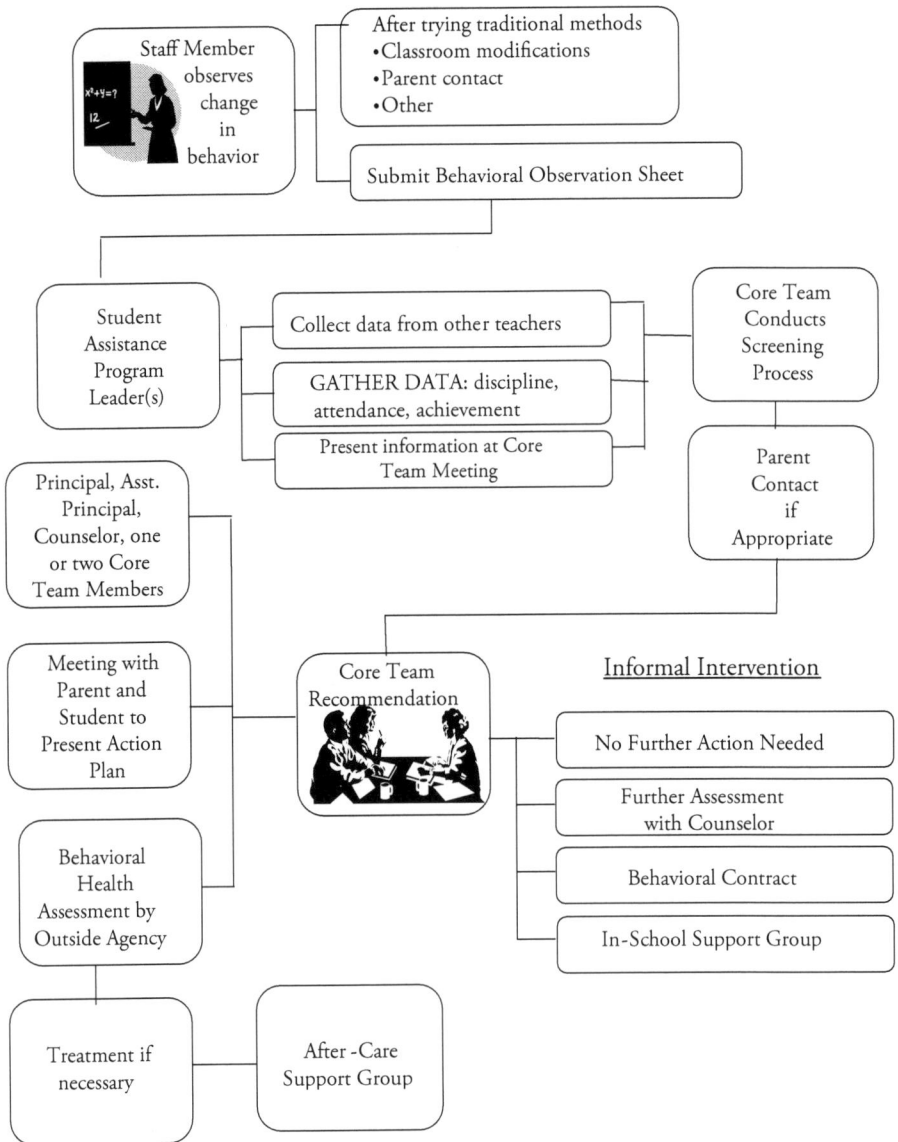

The SAP was cited as one of the most effective school-based prevention and early intervention programs (*Prevention Plus II*, Office of Substance Abuse Prevention, U.S. Department of Health and Human Services. Below, are the benefits of a successful SAP:

## Benefits of a Student Assistance Program

Decreases discipline referrals
Provides a violence prevention strategy
Promotes a safe learning environment
Reduces truancy and absenteeism
Provides a framework to connect existing resources
Helps teachers, administrators, and counselors by taking a team approach to solving problems that hinder a student's academic success
Creates meaningful partnerships between school, community resources, parents, and students

## How to Implement the Student Assistance Program

## Core Team Training

The best way to implement the SAP is to adequately train the Core Team, which will function as the school-wide referral process. This training in which I provide, fully prepares team members in their role, as well as implementation strategies. Having the entire team trained also provides an opportunity to promote team development and accelerate the implementation process. This training is usually provided on-site, and should be open to district faculty who need to understand the SAP When possible it is great to include community resources that may serve in a collaborative role. Through collaboration with state and national student association organizations, the following standards have been adopted as best practices. They are not a requirement, but they are suggested.

# Do it with Fidelity

The following standards are designed to ensure the integrity and effectiveness of Student Assistance Programs is maintained at a high level, maximizing the opportunity to help students.

**Minimum Two Day Training for Team**—individuals who serve on the Core Team need to attend training on the SAP identification and referral process, including how to facilitate effective parent/student interventions and problem-solving strategies. This training should be at least two consecutive days in length.

**All Campus Staff Trained in Referral Process**—once the SAP is implemented on campus, *all staff, including teachers, administrators, support staff,* etc., need to be oriented to how the Core Team functions, it's composition, and how referrals are initiated and processed. This is often done by the core team, either in staff meetings or one-on-one.

**Broad-Brush Approach With All Students Served**—any student demonstrating evidence of problems may be referred to the SAP, including students who eventually end up needing special education services or 504 accommodations. The SAP serves as an excellent pre-referral screening for students, regardless of the nature of the problem.

**Referrals Based On Observable Behaviors**—referrals from the classroom and other areas at school should be based on *patterns* of grades dropping, poor attendance, and or classroom behavior. Exceptions to this are parental and self-referrals. The primary tool for referrals based on observable, measurable data is the *Behavior Observation Sheet (BOS)*, a listing of behaviors often indicating that some sort of problem exists.

**Student Strengths & Interests Identified**—important in the screening process (the gathering of teacher observations) is the need to include student strengths on the BOS. In addition, the team can help the student get involved in things that interest him or her.

**Team Meets Routinely**—In order to develop effectively as a team, and to keep up with referrals, the team should meet regularly, either once a week or at the very least twice a month. In the initial phase of implementation, the Core

Team needs to meet weekly until all members are clear on the referral process. Teams that meet "as needed only", seldom reach a point of efficiency.

**SAP Team Coordinator**—the Core Team needs to be led by a designated coordinator who has been formally trained in the SAP Core Team process. This is often an administrator or grade level counselor. Make note that many classroom teachers make exceptional SAP coordinators; the personality has much to do with leadership style.

**District Coordinator**—the district needs to designate an SAP Coordinator who works to assist individual campuses with issues related to the overall district SAP efforts. This position needs to ensure that procedural consistency and community collaboration occur, particularly in the area of community-based assessments. This position ensures the SAP gets the clout needed to make an impact.

**School and Community Resources Identified**—The Core Team should be familiar with the existing campus resources that are designed to assist students, such as counseling, support groups, mentoring, conflict resolution, classroom modifications, etc. It is equally as important that the team be knowledgeable of the community-based resources that provide *free behavioral health assessments* to parents seeking help for their children, as well as other services such as food and clothing banks, medical resources, emergency financial assistance, etc.

**Non-diagnostic Support Services Offered**—students should be able to receive assistance without being diagnosed by the Core Team. Based on the observable and measurable indicators, often the school will be aware that a problem exists, yet have no clear idea of exactly what the problem is affecting the student. At no time does the SAP Core Team diagnose a student.

**Behavioral Health Assessments Offered**—in order to determine and address those issues beyond the school's capabilities (addiction, abuse, depression, etc.) community-based behavioral health assessments should be available to parents/students seeking assistance. This assessment should be at *no charge* and any decisions regarding participation and outcome should be the responsibility of the parent and/or students. By creating this collaborative bridge, schools help students and families get connected to local services, but without making the school liable. Any decision to seek help beyond the initial assessment is totally up to the parents. The school holds no decision making role.

**Parent and Student Awareness Offered**—once implemented, parents and students should be made aware of the SAP, how to seek assistance, and who is on the team. This is accomplished through letters to parents, brochures, student handbook, announcements, local newspaper articles, etc. Without adequate awareness, few parent referrals will be made.

**Evaluation Process**—the SAP needs to be evaluated annually, with attention placed on how the process impacts the referred student and the overall campus. In addition, the SAP process needs to be evaluated to determine where referrals are being generated and what kind of strategies the Core Team is utilizing. An *annual report* sent to the campus principal and district superintendent is essential for growth and expansion.

**Coordinating Framework or Platform**—a comprehensive, broad-brushed SAP needs to integrate seven key areas at school and the community. These elements are prevention, identification, screening, intervention, assessment, treatment, and support services. Essential to the success of the SAP is the understanding that the assessment and treatment elements are the responsibility of the community and parents, not the school.

**School Board Policy Established**—this guarantees that the SAP will receive the support and endorsement needed to exist within a school district. The policy should include purpose of the SAP and procedures needed to ensure effective functioning on all campuses.

## Summary

What becomes self-evident is that as models change, so do the objectives. Expectations of a core team are going to differ from those of an SAP counselor. They exist for different reasons. An effective SAP should demonstrate measurable school-related outcomes, including increased attendance, improved productivity, fewer repeat discipline referrals, and fewer drop outs. In addition, a SAP should result in students getting the opportunity to enter treatment when needed; it should connect families to existing community resources; it should make a difference. Stopping a student's emotional bleeding brought on by trauma, tragedy or disease is essential to academic success. The SAP is proven to do just that. Helping students' succeed is our primary mission. That is not rocket science.

*Unless someone like you cares a whole awful lot,*
*nothing is going to get better.*
*It's not.*
**Dr. Seuss**

# Chapter 25

# Wrapping it Up

Individuals can make a tremendous difference when it comes to interventions. The ability for a classroom teacher to effectively redirect behavior allows for a more nurturing class, hence more learning. The willingness of an administrator to leverage a student into making positive choices increases the chance of success for that student and family. A SAP team works effectively with resistant parents helping to provide specific information and support. But, without a clear systematic approach to interventions, the slings and arrows that strike our children will take their toll.

Idleness only contributes toward the problems. Standing back, either hoping someone else will step up or arrogantly claiming "it ain't my problem' won't help. We are our brother's keepers, because if we aren't who will be our keeper when the day comes.

Family problems, chemical dependency, depression, trauma, loss and all the other roadblocks our kids encounter aren't going away. Today's toddlers will soon arrive at the school-house door, wide-eyed and full of wonder. The challenges they face will be met with varying degrees of success. Most students will show up, apply themselves and generally succeed. But, there will always be those who need our help by providing them structure and redirection. Because if left unto their own devices, too many dreams will fade, and their names will be forgotten and their potential sadly missed.

This book is offered as a "toolbox" aiding the educator in the enormous job of educating children. By adding these tools to the tool belt, more time can be devoted to putting energy into why children come to school in the first place, to learn. Certainly interventions don't meet all the needs, just as prevention strategies alone are doomed to fail. There must be a concerted effort between schools, families, communities, and students.

Against all odds, many teachers have done what others say is impossible. Out there are men and women who not only trudge through the muck and mire of mandates, but are able to somehow float above it enough to reach out and connect with most students. Within this book are some of the methods that can help anyone connect to a student. But, this book does not contain what it takes to reach the heart of a teacher. Caring, thoughtful and deliberate intervention skills result from a myriad of moments, hours, days and years of experience. If there was a way to adequately capture in words how well many teachers do, this book would have an abundance of pages.

## Words from Mother Theresa

People are often unreasonable, illogical, and self-centered;
Forgive them anyway.
If you are kind, people may accuse you of selfish, ulterior motives;
Be kind anyway.
If you are successful, you will win some false friends and some true enemies;
Succeed anyway.
If you are honest and frank, people may cheat you;
Be honest and frank anyway.
What you spend years building, someone could destroy overnight;
Build anyway.
If you find serenity and happiness, they may be jealous;
Be happy anyway.
The good you do today, people will often forget tomorrow;
Do good anyway.
Give the world the best you have, and it may never be enough;
Give the world the best you've got anyway.
You see, in the final analysis, it is between you and God;
It was never between you and them anyway.

## Bad Things do happen to Good Kids, part 2

Continued from page 17

On her graduation day, Trish commented to a friend, "It is amazing I even got to high school", For a long time Trish was not sure she would; she was not sure she could; on top of that, she wasn't sure she even cared to. Thank God for the teachers who did; the teachers that made a huge difference; they may have even saved her life.

Her home life did not improve as she got older, it just changed; different monsters, but the same old fears. She wonders, "What if mom gets really hurt the next time?" "How long will Jimmy and I have to hide in closets?" Out of chronic terror, Trish hid well, so well she did not notice that the closets changed over the years. Different apartments and houses but from the inside, in the dark, all closets look pretty much the same.

By third grade, Trish had learned self-protection. She was not a cruel child, so she didn't lash out. She was not an angry child, and she didn't rage. However, she was a lonely child and like all lonely children yearned for closeness, for someone to understand. As other children seemed to play, Trish pulled back, observed the laughter and felt a vague sort of hurt somewhere in her stomach. She knew that feeling well. Other kids did notice Trish. They saw her isolating and distancing herself from others. She rarely spoke up when addressed, which was rare in itself. Trish even chose to look at the floor, ceiling or a wall, instead of make eye contact. When her teacher addressed her, it was as if Trish had gone somewhere and left her sad part behind. Her fourth grade teacher would call on Trish and then ridicule her for bowing her head and mumbling. It horrified Trish when called upon. Her teacher, who evidently was in the wrong profession, referred to Trish with words like "stupid and idiot". This always elicited giggles from the teacher's favorite students.

Somewhere between fourth and fifth grade, Trish got angry; angry with her mother for bringing bad men home, angry with Jimmy for his need for protection, and was angry with school because no one cared. Unknown to her, Trish was particularly angry with herself for being, in her words, "weird, dumb and ugly". The actions of others painted Trish in very false colors.

Trish told no one about how she felt. She assumed she was broken and could not be fixed. She wondered why other kids weren't. Her anger translated into secret behavior, like placing a tack on the seat of a student's desk when no one was looking, or writing nasty words in other students' books. One day when alone in the science classroom, Trish opened the cage with the white mice, letting them all out. This was done out of anger, but down deep inside she was pleased to set the rodents free. On the outside, Trish was quiet, reserved, passive, unassuming and awkward. On the inside, she was angry, confused defeated, alone, and just mean to herself.

In fifth grade, Trish had a teacher who noticed her lack of motivation, indifference to poor performance and what looked to be a sad emptiness inside. She also noticed how other students' treated Trish. They spewed out words such as "shabby, dull and ugly", called her "poor white trash" and ostracized her at every chance. School was a prison yard that ate her spirit and spit it out like rancid old meat. There was nowhere to go; home life was horrible and school became a lifeless cold place. Trish saw her life in a pitch-dark closet, with no way out. Ms. Sanchez, who apparently was in the right profession, grew concerned. She noticed the cruel way Trish's peers treated her. She observed a malicious gang of girls seeming to relish seeing Trish's hurt face. At lunch, she saw the girls telling Trish that she was not allowed to sit at their table and that she needed to find a table for "those without fashion or brains."

Quickly, Ms. Sanchez stepped in and did for Trish what no one had done before. She stood up for her; she treated Trish with kindness and patience. She gave Trish a safe place to hang out when she was most vulnerable. To Trish's amazement and relief, she saw an adult take action to protect her. Up to that moment, Trish had always been the one providing protection.

Ms. Sanchez took administrative action and was able to intervene with the bullying. Trish was empowered with choices and responsibilities in ways that fanned the spark of life that was almost extinguished. School began to feel safe again; not quite a sanctuary, but she no longer dreaded showing up. But, wounds go deep and scars remain; destructive patterns can be very persistent. There was still an internal rage that Trish was unable to keep buried. Smoldering all the time, it did not take much to set her off. Trish would sometimes react to situations that had nothing to do with her. Most of her rage though, was reflected inward, where it slowly consumed her. Trish needed help that went beyond what she could do. Even the best teachers have limitations on what can be done for students. It would be a while before her behavior and grades improved. It would be a while for the light in her eyes to come back on.

Concluding that Trish needed more help, her Ms. Sanchez referred her to the school's early intervention team where help was available. Within two weeks, Trish's mother met with Ms. Sanchez, her counselor and principal. The result of what is now regarded as monumental meeting resulted in Trish's involvement in a campus-based support group and her mother's agreement to schedule an assessment with a local professional in the community. Mom did not know this assessment would offer her help as well. Subsequently, mom was referred to a battered women's program and the family began a long and wondrous journey that was long overdue. Trish, Jimmy and mom started counseling together. Trish saw her home life change, her mom happier, her little brother safer and her days much better. Difficult mornings now were now evidenced with normal problems like not finding a shoe, or having her favorite outfit in the dirty clothes. No one referred to Trish as shabby and dull anymore, even though there were rare days when she felt herself drifting back to that more familiar life. Overshadowing all of this was the loveliest fact that birthdays truly became special days, mom stopped dating abusive men, and closets were for keeping clothes in safe storage, the kind of "safe" they were made for.

As the years passed, life continued to have its usual ups and downs. School was for a while a challenge and Trish throughout high school often felt awkward around peers. She fell in love for the first time and like so many young people, had her heart broken. She survived only to incidentally break the hearts of several young men. Most days were uneventful, even boring at times. But, storms still come; thunder roars and rains fall hard. Like all storms do, they eventually pass, leaving behind the promise of a clear and bright tomorrow.

## To Return

When the most sea-worthy ship is tossed by tempest storm
And, fury drives waves in violent, wicked form
The winds howl, skies grow dark but your rudder never fails
The safety of home-harbor would silent tattered sails
With miles behind and more to go the ship begins to list
The young onboard are hard to find when hidden by the mist
Sometimes they fall beyond your reach, their hands a bit too low
The sea is so angry, she captures many, she may never let them go
When morning time breaks and safe harbor is in sight
And, dark cloud fade to God's brilliant light
You know you'll go back, a sailor you'll be
Some people are just born to return to the sea

## In Closing

An educator's intuition, skill and technique cannot be overvalued. The relationship between a teacher and a student is tremendously important. When these factors are blended, amazing things take place, resulting in an experience where excitement, motivation, safety, learning and growth abound. However, the most seasoned and confident teacher can have moments of doubt about how to respond. Not responding is self-evident in its inadequacy and outcome. Young people rely upon adults to provide boundaries, consequences, gestures, recognition, validation and redirection. The language students speak is sometimes loud, crude, defiant, resistant and offensive; and, it is often reserved, desperate, whispered, hidden and camouflaged with behavior. As adults, we can see and hear their stories, or miss the messages, wondering why a student is difficult and challenging. My intent is to provide the reader with ideas, insights, suggestions, cautions and encouragements; expecting these pages to be regularly referenced and dog-eared.

## End of the Day

*After the day is done, in the silence of our prayers,*

*We come together for their sake.*

*For when it is truly measured, and all else falls away . . .*

*It is about the children.*

*For they are yours*

*For they are ours.*

*Thank You,*
*Noel R Love*

Noel Love
713-447-5989
noel@clark-love.com

**To order additional copies of this book, contact:**
Xlibris Corporation
1-888-795-4274
www.Xlibris.com
Orders@Xlibris.com

Printed in Great Britain
by Amazon